PEACE MAKERS

*A path for imperfec
people making peace
in an imperfect world*

Tools for
Effective Christian
Leadership

JIM ABRAHAMSON

🔥 Torchflame Books

This book is dedicated to my family,
my faithful wife Ceecy, my special son Daniel,
my delightful daughter Debbie, and my adventurous son David.
I am proud of them, often learning from them,
and always thankful for them.

Contents

Preface

Peace Makers is the second in a two part series and must be understood in the context of the first book, *Peace Seekers*. Originally the two books were to be one, and they should be read as part of a single thesis. *Peace Seekers* is not complete without *Peace Makers,* and *Peace Makers* is built upon the foundation of *Peace Seekers*. These books are about the relationship between God's grace in Christ and peace—personal inner peace and social outer peace.

As humans we are marked by three personal inner longings. We seek security, significance, and serenity. In *Peace Seekers* I have argued that inner serenity (peace) is a spiritual matter that cannot be fully experienced without addressing spiritual / theological issues. At the root of the psychological dissonance that we face is a conscience that calls us to ideals that we seem unwilling or unable to live by. Some have attempted to resolve the tension between the "ought" and the "actual" by attacking religious moral codes as the problem. They have felt that if we can rid our lives of expectations coming from outside our "true self," we will find peace. But humans seem to be hard wired with moral impulses that are difficult to remove. Part of our "true self" seems to include a theological connection with a moral agenda as a component.

Christianity has addressed the problem of inner peace in a different way. It embraces the Biblical moral law as holy and understands the human conscience as a part of God's image stamped on individuals making them distinct from lower forms of animal life. Without personal holiness man will not have fellowship with a holy God and there will be no real peace. We must be reconciled to God not vice versa. But what is the nature of the holiness that reconciles us to God and brings rest to our souls? Many Christians have believed that it is a holiness that is derived from a disciplined life of obedience empowered by the grace of God and the indwelling Spirit of Christ. In *Peace Seekers* I have argued that while such a life is admirable and encouraged, it is not sufficient to satisfy the high moral calling of God's law or our conscience. The standard for fellowship with God and rest for our souls is so high that no human has or can achieve it save one—Jesus Christ. The Gospel message is that only one person had to live the perfectly holy life. The good news is that the benefits of that life are made available to any and all who by faith are united with Christ. In *Peace Seekers* I have argued that the path to inner peace starts with respect for the high standards of a holy God who demands perfection. But I have also argued that there are no perfect people or perfect environments, only a perfect Messiah. The Christian Gospel is not focused on good sheep but on a Good Shepherd who imputes his righteousness to all who are united with him by faith. *"He made Him who knew no sin to be sin on our behalf, so that we might become the righteousness of God in Him."* 2 Corinthians 5:21. This is the gospel that Jesus secured, Paul taught, and that Christians proclaim today.

I believe faith that is vibrant, alive, abiding, and life changing must have a number of qualities. It must be rooted in the Gospel of grace. It must be intellectually convincing. It must be emotionally satisfying. It must be morally transforming. It must be socially connecting. It must be culturally inspiring. My aim in both *Peace Seekers* and *Peace Makers* is to encourage such a faith in my readers' lives. In *Peace Seekers* I wanted to provide the foundation for deep peace of mind and soul by addressing and relieving a profound, inner, moral dissonance in life. In *Peace Makers* I want to show how the gospel of radical grace can impact society. The book you are about to read is not a book on social political strategies or psychological tools for social reform. It is rather a foundation for both. It is a way of seeing God and those made in His image. This perspective is a necessary component to social change, interpersonal reconciliation, and peacemaking. I believe that its thesis, which is the radical grace of God bringing personal inner peace leading to social peace, is too often ignored or naively assumed. I want to change that.

Introduction

"I came not to bring peace but, a sword." These words do not come from Mohammed. They are found in Matthew 10:34 as the words of Jesus. In the context of Matthew's Gospel they point to the trouble followers of Christ will experience in this world. They will experience division, strife, and conflict even in their own families. This runs contrary to the popular notion that God's people should expect to experience a path that is free from social turmoil and pain. Whatever peace Christ offers, it is for imperfect people in an imperfect world. It is peace in a storm.

But there is another context in which Jesus brings a sword rather than peace. Jesus brought a sword in the sense that he would slay the self-confident and self-sufficient spirit of all who ignore or domesticate the moral demands of a holy God. Jesus calls us to find peace and make peace by sharing his cross—dying in some sense to our own merit or ability. In order to experience the resurrection power of the Prince of Peace and reconcile social relationships, we must experience the "death of", "preoccupation with", and "confidence in" our own spiritual self-sufficiency. This is the repentance that leads to eternal life. He would bring death to us so that we might find life in him as we are united with him by faith. The irony is that when we seek to find our lives, we lose them; and when we lose them in Christ, we find them. We are literally dying to live.

The path to inner peace leads first to the holy Law of Moses where we are broken before God's high moral demands. The path then turns to the foot of the cross of Christ where we find grace and peace apart from our own moral merit. And finally it calls for a response of faith in Christ. If we are to be peacemakers, we must first find peace in Christ through brokenness before the law, atonement through the cross, and the obedience of faith. The first book in this series, *Peace Seekers,* as the foundation for *Peace Makers*, should be read as a part of the development of one common theme—grace that leads to peace. Peacemakers must first be peace seekers.

Social Peace is Rooted in Personal Peace.

How are we to understand the root of our many and complex social problems? Take crime for example. Suppose we find that poor people commit more crimes than rich people. Do we then conclude that poverty causes crime, and if we could reduce poverty, we would reduce crime? Or could it be that the same things that cause poverty also tend to cause crime? Correlation does not prove cause. The belief that because things occur together, one must cause the other is a common error, or logical fallacy. So how then do we understand the root cause of social problems? Does the Scripture shed any light on this challenging question?

Classical Greco-Roman ethics were principally concerned with justice and social applications—civil government, economic systems, family structure, etc. By way of contrast Christianity places more emphasis on love and personal ethics—the relationship of man to God as well as individual to individual. This is not to suggest that Jesus and the Apostles were not aware of or concerned with social institutions. They seem however to assume that personal ethics are fundamental and foundational to social systems.

The Apostle James links social ethics and peace to personal spiritual / psychological peace.

> *"What is the source of quarrels and conflicts among you? Is not the source your pleasures that wage war in your members? You lust and do not have; so you commit murder. And you are anxious and cannot obtain; so you fight and quarrel."*
> James 4:1–2

The experience of inner peace could well be the most important social issue of our times because of its critical role in political peace and moral discipline. The root source of social and psychological peace comes from somewhere other than our environment or our fallen

4

nature with its imperfect track record. Moral discipline, ethical responsibility, and social reform are in short supply but the path to these virtues must first pass through a deeply personal experience of peace.

Mahatma Gandhi, Abraham Lincoln, Martin Luther King Jr., Nelson Mandela, and many other champions of social reconciliation were men and women whose freedom from bitterness did not come from their outward circumstances but from an inner peace that empowered them to change their world. Not all of these individuals were Christians but each of them found their inspiration and power from the Christian message. They recognized Jesus not as a political activist but rather as a visionary moral prophet who linked social reform to personal inner renewal. The notion that inner peace demands a perfect environment and/or perfect people is misguided. Attempts to manage the environment, thinking that this alone would bring deep psychological peace and social harmony, is misguided. James reminds us that personal inner change comes before and is key to outer social change. Outer turmoil and social evil are the fruit of personal unrest. The experience of God's grace is a prerequisite to the expression of God's grace. We love because He first loved us. Communities of peace are made up of people who are at peace with God, others, and themselves.

As with *Peace Seekers* my goal in writing this book is to inspire reform by laying the foundation for it. My aim is to bring people to understand grace to the extent that they sense a new freedom that leads not just to inner peace and joy but also to social reconciliation. Peacemakers are not just political pacifists with Jesus as their inspiration. If you are expecting a study of political strategies for peacemaking in this book, you may at first be disappointed; but I trust that in the end you will be rewarded. *Peace Makers* lays the most needed and often neglected inner foundation for the peacemaking process.

In *Peace Seekers* we looked at what God had done in Christ to bring peace to imperfect people in an imperfect world. It pointed to the importance of evaluating life in spiritual / moral terms noting that our greatest anxieties are rooted in our broken relationship with God. It went on to explain a New Covenant way of looking at our lives. This New Covenant in Christ reconciled us to God even when we were not perfect. This new relationship frees us from the condemnation of the Law of Moses, a law that had the effect of breaking us and leaving us powerless to escape our condition of anxiety, fear, and shame. The book concluded by addressing the role of faith, which is instrumental to bringing the benefits of Christ's work to us. The good news of the Gospel of Christ is that the blessings of peace are by grace through faith apart from our moral reform and apart from the reformation of a broken world.

In *Peace Makers* we continue to develop some of the implications embedded in the grace of the Gospel. *Peace Seekers* was not about psychology, and *Peace Makers* is not about politics although both include implications for both disciplines. The idea that ties the two books together is this – When we embrace the radical grace of God in Christ, it provides a basis for inner psychological peace that frees us to demonstrate grace in social relationships so as to foster social peace.

Who Should Read this Book?

Like *Peace Seekers* this book is written for those who want reconciliation with God, self, and others. It is written for those who need to understand, embrace, and express the radical grace of God in Christ. It is written for those who want to be peacemakers in the world but are frustrated by a lack of inner resources to do so. Whereas *Peace Seekers* gave attention to the formation of personal inner peace, *Peace Makers* will give more attention to the power of grace and inner peace to affect one's relationship with the outer world. It will address the question—How can I demonstrate to others the radical grace of God in Christ?

Three groups of people will profit from reading this book—first, those who need help in experiencing and expressing the grace of God, second, those who want to minister to them, and third, those who seek to play a vital role in conflict resolution. Leaders can also profit from *Peace Makers* as they model lives of grace and peace, teaching others to constructively resolve conflicts.

A Dangerous Book

The radical grace of God can be misunderstood and abused. In some cases people have used it as an excuse for self-serving, sinful, and worldly behavior. But the radical love and grace I will so often reference is Paul's message, which he identified and defended as the gospel. Paul recognized that if his readers correctly understood his teaching, they would logically ask the question, *"Should we sin that grace may abound?"* (Rom. 6:1.) In response to this question, Paul does not exhort his readers to recommit their lives to moral discipline under the law; he rather underscores the wonderful, new relationship they have with God through faith expressed in their baptism. What many of us need is not more of the law but a better understanding of grace. Paul was convinced that the grace and love of God were the greatest motivators for godly responses to life. There is another reason this book might be dangerous. Not only might it give some an excuse to be morally irresponsible, it might lead people to believe that social justice is unimportant. Those who read the third section of this book will be challenged to recognize that a demand for justice may be an obstacle to real social peace. I do not want to suggest that social activism in support of justice for those who are abused is unimportant. I am suggesting that before we go there, we need to deal with the demand for justice in our own personal lives.

But don't we already understand grace? The answer is simple. In spite of all that has been said and penned on the Grace of God, I find that people continue to misunderstand it, seldom experience it, and too rarely show it. While God's grace in Christ can be misrepresented, and it often is; it cannot be overemphasized. Because it is so often resisted, it must be a persistent point of emphasis in the Christian's life and message. It must be framed and modeled in ways that permit its power to transform our lives and the lives of all who meet us.

Jesus' prayer for all his followers in John 17:26 is that *"the love wherewith Thou didst love me may be in them."* It is the infusion of this love from God that motivates the changing of our lives and the writing of this book. When we know we are significant and secure as His children and when we sense His love for those around us, we are transformed and we become peacemakers.

How Is this Book Structured?

Peace Makers is structured around three biblical stories that depict God's love and grace. Each story features a contrasting pair of individuals. First, we look at two sisters in Luke 10—Martha and Mary. They will help us see the relationship of worship to work in the context of grace. Second, we will move to the story of two sons in Luke 15—the prodigal and his brother where we will examine the dynamics of repentance and grace. In the third section we will look at Matthew 18 and see two lenders—one gracious and the other unmerciful. They will help us see the relationship between grace and graciousness.

Each of the three sections will begin with an introduction and a self-test designed to prepare the reader to appreciate the chapters that follow. Each section will include a chapter(s) prescribing a step to experiencing and expressing grace and peace followed by a chapter(s) dealing with an obstacle to peace. At the end of each chapter will appear a series of application responses and/or discussion questions.

Like *Peace Seekers*, *Peace Makers* covers some familiar ground in a fresh way. It will remind the reader of core teachings of the Christian faith that are easily forgotten. Some of the material that I present is controversial, but I hope not confusing. I want my readers to understand and believe that the biblical message is the gospel of grace—radical, risky, unbelievable grace. I also want my readers to feel the heart of God and open themselves to the many ways in which God deals with His people. And finally I want people to know what grace in action looks like. I want them to see how a gracious life lives in the real world of family, church, work, and play. But most of all I want the Apostle Paul's prayer for all of us to be answered *"that the eyes of our hearts would be enlightened so that we would know what is the hope of Christ's calling for us, what are the riches of the glory of His inheritance in us, and the greatness of God's power toward us."*

The Message of this Book in a Nut Shell

A quick review of the first three steps and obstacles from the book *Peace Seekers* will set the context for *Peace Makers*.

Step #1 The spirit of **Holiness** - embracing Jesus' teachings about holiness and being broken by them.

Obstacle #1 A **Lawless** spirit - building a foundation of self-sufficiency that does not understand the just demands of a holy God.

Step #2 The **New Covenant** spirit - moving our eye away from our personal moral merit to what God has done for us in Christ.

Obstacle #2 A **Legalistic** spirit - inviting us to live under the Law will keep us from peace and peacemaking.

Step #3 The spirit of **Faith** - receiving the righteousness of Christ available to us. It is a righteousness that is first available *for* us and then *in* and *through* us.

Obstacle #3 An **Independent** spirit - looking for hope in anything and everything but God will rob us of peace and effective peacemaking.

Peace Makers adds three more steps and obstacles to peace with a focus on peacemaking.

The points expressed in this book are an addition to and a continuation of the three steps and obstacles in the first book in this series—*Peace Seekers*. Personal peace that comes through God's grace empowers us to make peace in social relationships.

Step #4 The spirit of **Sabbath** - integrating God's Rest into our everyday lives.

Obstacle #4 A spirit of **busyness** - confusing work with our worth blocks personal peace and peacemaking.

Step #5 The spirit of **repentance** - turning our pain into insight that leads us home.

Obstacle #5 A spirit of **religion** – with its scorekeeping, separatist, and superficial posture will block peace and peacemaking.

Step #6 The spirit of **empathy** - reminding us of the grace that has been shown to us, and its need to be shown by us to others.

Obstacle #6 A spirit of **justice** - demanding one's rights will keep us from personal peace and effective peacemaking.

Section I

Grace and Worship

The Story of Two Sisters:
Mary and Martha

Grace inspires and frees us to bring a spirit of worship to our work without making work the object of our worship.

A prominent Christian physician confessed that he was expected to work 80 hours per week. He felt justified in keeping such a schedule because he was serving a vital need. But whose need was it? Could it have been *his need* for significance? We live in a culture that tends to worship at work, work at play, and play at worship. What does it mean to worship at work? We worship at work when it becomes the place where we make our greatest sacrifices, find our greatest significance, and experience our deepest fulfillment in life. How many families have suffered neglect at the hand of a father or mother who has sacrificed the bulk of their time and passion at the altar of vocational goals. When a culture gives so much attention to productivity and attaches such powerful financial and emotional rewards to "success" in the workplace, it will produce more than goods and services. It will also produce workaholics—people who worship at work. It is embarrassing to see this tragic pattern played out even in Christian service. Christians who sacrifice family and health to find personal security, significance, and serenity in "ministry" are bowing to a pagan culture more than the Kingdom of God. In the process they will neither find peace nor make peace.

Much of our secular vocation and religious activity while looking like virtuous commitment in reality may reflect something less noble. Work can be an effective painkiller or distraction from the restlessness that terrorizes our souls. We may be making our work the basis of our worth, which is worshiping our work or ourselves through our work. In vocation / ministry sometimes it is not our busyness for God but rather our quiet faithfulness that is most important. Radical grace calls us to a "Sabbath" of the soul before it encourages us to a life of dutiful service. It is easy to recognize that busyness is not the place to find peace. The motivation for and quality of our labor is far more important to God than our busyness. Being busy "serving the Lord" does not mean we are "following Jesus" or glorifying God.

Jesus gives us a window into the nature of radical grace and the peace it produces in Luke 10 where He tells the story of two sisters, Mary and Martha. Martha is a classic illustration of "worship at work." Mary will show us something that may look like a shrugging of responsibility, but her choices win the commendation of Jesus.

Luke 10:38–42

"As Jesus and his disciples were on their way, he came to a village where a woman named Martha opened her home to him. She had a sister called Mary, who sat at the Lord's feet listening to what he said. But Martha was distracted by all the preparations that had to be made. She came to him and asked, "Lord, don't you care that my sister has left me to do the work by myself? Tell her to help me!" "Martha, Martha," the Lord answered, "you are worried and upset about many things, but only one thing is needed. Mary has chosen what is better, and it will not be taken away from her."

What a powerful and perplexing message this story sends. Martha is the gracious host who ministers to Jesus by "opening her home" to Him. Hospitality was (and is) an important virtue in Eastern cultures, and those who practiced it were to be commended. Not only does she open her home, she is also responsible in the tangible service she provides to her guests. There were preparations that "had to be done." She was not about to neglect these responsibilities. Furthermore Martha was fully aware that it was not culturally becoming of a Jewish woman to be taught the things of God. Mary's proper place was not in the study but in the kitchen with Martha.

Martha was one of those people who worked hard to do the right thing and expected others to do the same—particularly her sister. In her frustration Martha sees her sister as insensitive, irresponsible, inappropriate, and immature. Martha comes to Jesus and seems surprised that Jesus is not noticing Mary's delinquency, so she reminds him of Mary's responsibility to help her. It is obvious Martha has great respect for Jesus and every expectation that he will correct Mary. It is also obvious that she sees her ministry task as a burden she would rather not do alone. You can almost hear her envy of Mary: "I wish I could sit around all day and chat like Mary, but if I don't do this, it won't get done." Jesus' gentle response, "Martha, Martha," is one of loving concern. Martha must have been shocked by His words. But not only Martha, everyone who hears this story must be amazed at what the Lord said: "*Only one thing is needed.*" What is Jesus trying to say? These words remind me of Jesus' reply to Satan in Matthew 4:4 where He says: "*Man cannot live by bread alone but by every word that proceeds from the mouth of God.*" Could Martha be the one needing correction?

Shouldn't we all be applauding Martha? Can we appreciate Martha's frustration? She has been left with the hard work of the ministry while Mary is seemingly oblivious to Martha's burden. Some might say Mary acts like the typical spectator, consumer of our culture. Mary is receiving while Martha is giving. But as Jesus points out, there are some things more important than "working for the Lord." And in this story the "good thing" is neglected, as Martha is "*distracted with all her preparations.*" Radical grace challenges us with this simple question: In all of our busyness are we really doing the good thing? Faith is a verb to be expressed in action, but it is a mistake to demand that it be only a verb reducing Christianity to ethics—personal and social reform, or public service.

In the upcoming section we will explore the relationship between grace, worship, and ministry. We will learn in some cases it is better to receive than to give. Martha will show us that good work done for a good reason is no virtue if it displaces a more important activity. We will learn that the agenda of the kingdom of God is more than just being busy doing good things in service of God. It is more than a missional focus. Mary will teach us to bring a perpetual Sabbath spirit to our life and work. We will learn that Martha's kitchen is not a bad place to be if we can serve from a grace-filled posture.

Mary	*Martha*
Worship	Work (busyness)
The greater thing	The distraction
Our first calling	Our second calling
The 1st commandment	The 2nd commandment
Is seen as irresponsible by Martha	Sees herself as a victim
A picture of peace	A picture of stress

There is a lot to learn from these two sisters. Mary's example shows us that the Sabbath is more than a special day of rest; it is a lifestyle of spiritual peace. Martha's example reveals a common obstacle to peace in life. Her busyness and ours can be a powerful distraction from our first calling—a life of worship—and the peace that comes from walking in it. And it is not only personal peace that is at stake in this worship / work relationship. Peacemakers start by modeling a lifestyle that calls those who know them to worship but not at work.

Before we look at the lessons from these two sisters, let's see to what extent we might be a spiritual child of Martha or Mary. Circle (a) or (b), whichever seems most accurate to you.

1.

(a) The biggest problem in our church is a lack of responsible Christian workers.

(b) The greatest problem in our church is a lack of thankfulness to and faith in God.

2.

(a) I view praise and worship as a "pre-game warm-up" to a sermon that will exhort all of us to live a responsible Christian life.

(b) I look forward to worship when I meet with others on Sunday, and I expect to be motivated by a message that will remind me of what God has done in Christ.

3.

(a) I believe God's work will get done on His timetable.

(b) I feel like I am the only one volunteering around here.

4.

(a) I feel free to smell the roses even when there is work yet to be done.

(b) The demands of life often overwhelm me.

5.

(a) I don't understand how people can just sit around when there is so much work to be done.

(b) I am more concerned about developing a relationship with Christ than reaching ministry goals.

6.

(a) I spend a lot of time listening to God, other people, and my own soul.

(b) I have never been known as a good listener.

7.

(a) Too many people are so "spiritually" minded that they are insensitive to practical, "worldly" realities.

(b) Too many people are busy doing things for God and themselves while they don't seem to grow in their love for God and others.

8.

(a) My biggest challenge is to make time to meditate, listen, and appreciate God and others.

(b) Laziness is my biggest problem. I need to be more productive in ministry.

9.

(a) The Great Commission calls me to bear fruit (win people to faith) for the gospel of Christ.

(b) The Great Commission calls me to walk with God and sense His presence as I relate to others.

10.

(a) My motto is "Just do it."

(b) My motto is "Know yourself, accept yourself, die to yourself, and give yourself."

11.

(a) The big need in my life is more self-discipline.

(b) The greatest need in my life is more faith.

12.

(a) My greatest passion is to know Christ and make him known to others through my life.

(b) My passion is to serve the practical needs of others.

13.

(a) I want to know all I can about what Christ has done and what his kingdom is like.

(b) I have a real hard time with preachers who always talk about theology and don't emphasize practical service.

NOTE:

The (a) statements represent a life after the posture of Martha, except in #3,4,6,8,12,13 where it is the reverse.

Chapter 1
Mary, Mary, Quite Contrary

Step #4 to Peace with God:
Observe the Sabbath

*We experience peace with God when
we bring the Sabbath to our work.*

A devout Christian woman in our community was suffering from cancer and facing death. She had lived a faithful life of service and was respected by all who knew her for her faith and love for Christ. As her death became eminent, she expressed a number of concerns to me as her pastor—concerns about leaving her husband and children, concerns about the welfare of her various ministry activities, and concerns about her witness to others, especially those who did not confess faith in Christ. As I listened to her many concerns, I could not help but sense I was in the presence of the Martha of Jesus' day. I reminded this dear saint of God that all of the things she was concerned about were important, but the most important thing for her to do during the last days of her life was to sit at Jesus' feet as Mary did. She understood and found comfort in the story she knew and had taught to others. It is so easy to be busy in mind and body with the important responsibilities of life and to overlook the most important.

A.W. Tozer got it right when he noted, "Christians make a big mistake when they take a new convert and immediately make a worker out of him. Young believers first must be taught to worship, and only then will their work have God's fingerprints on it". To understand radical grace we need to understand it in the context of law. But we need to also understand it in the context of busyness. Grace first calls us to rest from our labor and toil so we can understand there are some things more important than being busy—even being busy for God.

Worship is a Reflective Response to God and Life.

As a child my parents told me, "Finish your work, then you can play." Play is for leisure; it is dessert; it is optional; it is really not so vital as work. Unfortunately we have sometimes viewed worship as a form of play. As I noted earlier: we worship at work, work at play, and play at worship. I think we sometimes believe God has the attitude—life is all about work. We wrongly assume He is first and foremost looking for workers for the harvest who will redeem the time, answer the call to make disciples, and multiply their talents. We forget Jesus' example of removing himself from the busyness of ministry to be alone with his Father. As a matter of fact I can't think of any examples of Jesus being in a hurry, being anxious, or being Martha like.

Traditional societies did not have the modern conveniences of our technology yet they seem to find the time to cultivate a culture of reflection and worship that we have lost in our rush to be productive, and efficient. Have we lost a respect for leisure as a time of worshipful, contemplative, reflection? A society that has no time for rest and reflection is in danger of loosing contact with its roots. The Genesis story of our human beginning orders the events in the following way. First, God creates, then God calls to worship, and finally God commands to work. Have we neglected this ordering of life?

A point to ponder

Worship comes AFTER God's work
and BEFORE our work.

Our modern worship services too often call us to work rather than cause us to reflect. For many Sunday has become a time to recharge for a week of work rather than a time to contemplate why we are doing what we are doing.

After a hard weeks work we expect to sleep in on Sunday or at least be entertained with music, sermons, and skits that compete with the rest of our society in trying to make us laugh, cry, or generally feel good.

We must not forget that worship is a reflective response to life. It is a response to God's work in creation and redemption. It is a contemplation of how we, as bearers of God's image, should respond to the opportunities, demands, and circumstances of life.

Bearing the fruit of the Spirit in the sense Jesus speaks of it in John 15 is best defined as abiding in Christ (the vine) and responding to the circumstances of life in a Godly way. It is significant to note the qualities that constitute a description of love in 1 Corinthians 13:4–6, and the fruits of the Spirit in Galatians 5:22–23 are nearly all *responses* to life. They are not descriptive of our production of anything tangible. It is offering a blessing to those who disappoint us or hurt us. It is showing love to those who are hard to love. It is giving credit to God and others when we are honored or rewarded. It is basking in the wonder of God's power and wisdom as we enjoy a sunset. It involves inner attitudes that only God sees. It does not have to produce or accomplish or solve or fix or do anything other than respond to life with a grateful heart, a listening ear, and the joy of experiencing God.

Worship is more important to God than our activity for Him. Or we should say, our activity for God, others, and ourselves should be an act of worship. We need to hear this message at a time when we tend to quickly equate activity with spiritual health. This message is also needed when we think of the need for "laborers in the harvest", or when we are sensitive to the "branch bearing fruit", "redeeming the time", and "investing our talents". Our actions may be little more than vain attempts to find meaning, a false hope in securing happiness, or a desperate measure to fulfill our duty. When we are properly preoccupied, the results will be seen in the character of our activity. There will be a spiritual fruitfulness that is measured not in time logged, projects completed, and people influenced, but in our response to life—love, joy, peace, patience, kindness, self-control, sensitivity, generosity, and so on.

Signs of a Healthy Church.

As a congregational consultant I have observed the inside workings of several churches and have established three ways to assess the health of a congregation. First, I look at relationships within the leadership. I have learned not to be impressed with busyness and activity—fifteen-hour work-days, ambitious plans, and high standards of outward excellence. What I do look at are the social and spiritual dynamics within the leadership of the church. Do staff members respect each other, love each other, and relate honestly and closely with each other? If the staff aren't experiencing close "fellowship", the congregation will probably not be led into deep "fellowship". The same is true of the lay leaders. What kind of relationship exists between staff leaders and lay leaders? Is there honest communication? Is there deep respect and love? Is there a growing sense of "community"? I look for radical grace in these relationships. I look for a pace of work that includes ample time for quality relationship building.

Second, I observe the worship service. I am not impressed with growth or size. I am not so concerned about the eloquence of the sermon, the quality of the music, the aesthetics of the space, or the orderliness of the meeting. I am interested in the congregation's body language. Are they excited about being together for worship? Do they indeed worship—get their attention off self and one another and on God? Do they show interest, care, and compassion for the immature, the burned out, and the wounded among them? Is there a sense of God's Spirit present in how they relate, what they talk about, and whom they embrace as part of the family? I look for relationships based on radical grace and expressed through gratitude toward God.

Third, I attend an annual meeting to watch and listen. I can tell a lot about a congregation by observing the way it handles decisions regarding money, staff, goals, and crises. I am not concerned with the size of the budget or how smoothly the presentations are made. I am looking to see if people are speaking freely and honestly with each other. Does the leadership listen, affirm, and encourage faith with good works? Can the leadership keep order without leaving people feeling they have been manipulated? Are people civil with each other? Are people appropriately thankful? I look for signs of radical grace in these relationships.

The true spirit of a church cannot be hidden from those who carefully observe the quality of relationships in the congregation. Some congregations pride themselves in the number of missionaries they support, the number of ministries they run, the number of people who attend, the quality of services they provide, and the level of activity they require of members. This "Martha's kitchen" stuff does not impress me if it is not deeply respectful of "Mary's posture". Activity for Jesus may be better than activity for some other things or no activity at all, but it is a far cry from our calling if a spirit of worship is not present.

In the biblical story of Mary and Martha there are two responses given to Martha by Jesus. First, He explained the virtue of Mary's choice and then second, He defended Mary's posture by refusing to be manipulated by Martha in her recruiting efforts. Jesus refused to "take away" Mary's good part lest she, like Martha, be preoccupied with ministry.

Mary Can Be a Pharisee.

One of the parables of Jesus comes to my mind when I think of Mary and Martha. It is the story of the Pharisee and the publican in Luke 18:9–14. The Pharisee takes an outward position not unlike that of Mary. He "fasts twice a week", "pays tithes", and "prays". But his problem is his pride in his actions. In his pride he looks down with

21

contempt at the tax-gatherer who is a sinner. It is not unusual in my experience to find folks who pride themselves in being Marys. They seem to find security in looking down on the Marthas of the world with contempt and even pity. After all we Marys are the truly spiritual lot.

I ask this question to Marys who are really Pharisees at heart. When you sit at the feet of Jesus, are you sure you are listening to Jesus and not to your carnal ego's press secretary? Be sure you are learning at the Master's feet and not just seeking to fulfill a spiritual duty or to get a spiritual high. Be assured of this: when our Lord sees a Pharisee at His feet, He still sees a Pharisee.

Signs can reveal when we have a Mary and not a Pharisee at Jesus' feet. Marys don't judge Marthas. Marys are so taken with confessing their own sins they have little time to notice, let alone confess the sins of others. Marys are not looking for fulfillment or a "spiritual high"; they are too interested in learning from Jesus and appreciating His presence. Marys are easy to edify and hard to distract with petty things, small thinking, and superficial details. Marys are not avoiding responsibility but are making grace and gratitude a higher responsibility than ministry. In chapter two of this book we will note the order of Romans 12 where service follows worship.

I Need to Find Myself.

A counselor has two responsibilities: 1) help the counselee accurately reflect on their story, and 2) help the counselee wisely respond to life's circumstances. The essence of spiritual formation can be captured in four phrases: know yourself, accept yourself, forget yourself, and give yourself. This may sound a little Freudian until we frame it in the context of the Gospel. Knowing ourselves is a lifelong process most of us never truly finish. One of the great obstacles to knowing ourselves is the fear we will not end up liking who we really are. Throughout our lives we have grown to accept and like an image of ourselves, but many fear that our self-image may be just a fantasy wish. The grace of God is vital if we are to explore our true identity without fear. As disciples of Jesus we are challenged to accept and then forget ourselves, but this is hardly possible if we do not know who we are.

One of the best-fed and well-protected "sacred cows" in our culture is the sacred cow of personal wholeness. After all, "I can't be expected to love you until I have learned to love myself." It is commonly understood that only after I find my life can I consider losing it for others. One of the most popular watering holes for our sagging self-image is work. Our work can easily take on a "Messianic role" as it gives our life meaning, governs our decisions, and medicates our wounds. Work, be it "secular" or "ministry," too often is the temple where we worship in that it is the place where our soul seeks to find its identity and worth. It does not help when our Christian friends applaud us for hard work and frown on us when we seem to withdraw from it.

At one time or another the kitchen is a good place for all of us to be, but when it comes to "finding ourselves," we will do better at Jesus' feet than toiling over the kitchen stove. The kitchen can be a hiding place where we stay distracted and avoid seeing God or ourselves. We will more often find ourselves while at Jesus' feet, quietly meditating on His Word and reflecting on life. It is in the context of a life "full on the inside" that we find spiritual power to minister on the outside. If this sounds like a luxury for only the rich who have time on their hands, you are right. When we are rich in the way Jesus was, we will have time even when we are in the kitchen of life. At this point you may be sensing that I am suggesting that an ascetic life is the goal of serious Christians. NO! That is not what I am suggesting. It is an ascetic spirit that I am calling for.

A lot of hurting people have come to our congregation. I often told them if they are here and are young in the faith, we do not expect them to serve but to learn. If they have been burned out in ministry, we ask them to rest and not serve. If they have been abused and mistreated, we will not ask them to work but to heal. And then after they have learned, rested, and healed, we will eventually expect them to teach, give rest to the weary, and heal others. We want people in Martha's kitchen who have Mary's heart.

The Sabbath of the Soul

Christians and Jews worship on different days as a testimony to different covenants—law and grace. The day of worship is a symbol of the covenant under which we live. Grace is acknowledged in our day of worship. The fact that the children of the New Covenant worshipped on Sunday, not Saturday as the Jews worship, is a testimony to the fact that the covenants have changed. There were three aspects of the Mosaic Covenant that were of particular importance to Israel. Three elements set Israel apart from the Gentile nations. The three elements were circumcision, dietary laws, and the Sabbath. The fact that these three issues are conspicuously absent under the administration of the New Covenant underscores the fact that the Old Covenant has been abrogated as a covenant. (See 1 Cor. 7:19; Rom. 2:25–29; 4:9–12; Gal. 2:3–5; 5; 2–6; 6:15; Phil. 3:3; Rom. 14–15; 1 Cor. 8–10; Gal. 2:11–14; Rom. 14:5–6; Gal. 4:10; and Col. 2:16–17.)

The way Paul treats the Sabbath provides a powerful illustration of the termination of the law as a covenant including the Ten Commandments. The Sabbath "as a holy day" is a symbol of the Old Covenant. By observing the Sabbath day, devout Jews were paying their deepest respect to the covenant God made through Moses. In Deuteronomy 5:13 we read, *"You shall remember that you were a slave in the land of Egypt, and that Yahweh your God brought you out with a strong hand and an outstretched arm; that is why Yahweh your God has commanded you to observe the Sabbath day."* This is underscored by the fact that there is no clear indication of Sabbath observance before Moses.

Nehemiah 9:13–14 also traces the initiation of Sabbath law to Moses and the Ten Commandments.

Strict observance of Sabbath law was fundamental to the Old Covenant. The demands and penalties for failure to observe the Sabbath were severe. *"Everyone who profanes it shall surely be put to death; for whoever does any work on it, that person shall be cut off from among his people"* (Ex. 31:14). Under the Maccabees (between the OT and NT), a group of Jews let themselves be slaughtered by the Syrians rather than put up active resistance and thus violate the Sabbath (1 Macc.2:32–38).

Jesus who was "born under the law" honored the Sabbath while challenging the man-made traditions that had grown to surround it. For example, the Pharisee of Jesus' day forbid men to carry a bed, to nurse a sick person, or to walk further than two thousand yards for fear of working on the Sabbath. Jesus rejected these man-made applications of the Sabbath law. But did Jesus intend His church to observe *a sacred day* of rest? Is the Sabbath to be *a day* of rest observed by God's people as a part of His moral mandate under the New Covenant?

I believe the New Covenant Sabbath is best understood as a "state of the soul" and not a sacred day for two reasons. First the word "Sabbath" means "to rest," and a full understanding of the teaching of the New Testament on this subject must include Hebrews four where the text explains there was more than a "day of the week" in view. *"For if Joshua had given them rest, He would not have spoken of another day after that. There remains therefore a Sabbath rest for the people of God. For the one who has entered His rest has himself also rested from his works, as God did from His"* (Heb.4:8–10). From the perspective of the New Covenant, the Sabbath was a picture of a spiritual condition or posture characterized by rest from work. In other words it was a life of faith, not a special day of restricted activity. The true Sabbath (under grace) is a "lifestyle" more than a "day." *"We who believe enter that rest."* 4:3. This is not to suggest that the free observation of a day of physical rest is unimportant. It simply means the issue under the New Covenant is not "a day" so much as "a spiritual posture." It means a person may be very serious and disciplined in keeping a Sabbath Day while completely ignoring the greater call to live a life of spiritual rest.

The second basis for the Sabbath as a state of the soul comes from Acts and the Epistles where there is no indication the Sabbath code of the Old Covenant was binding upon the church. This is consistent with what has already been observed with respect to the termination of the Mosaic covenant. With the end of the law there was freedom with respect to special days of worship in Paul's mind. Listen to what Paul says in Romans 14:5: *"One man regards one day above another, another regards every day alike. Let each man be fully convinced in his own mind."* In Colossians 2:16–17 Paul warns his readers, *"Therefore let no one act as your judge in regard to food or drink or in respect to a festival or a new moon or a Sabbath day – things which are a mere shadow of what is to come but the substance belongs to Christ."* In Galatians 4:9–10 he says much the same thing. Some interpreters make a distinction between the weekly Sabbath (which was mandated) and the special Sabbaths (which were not). Paul however does not make this distinction in his teaching.

The "Lord's Day," or Sunday, came to be recognized as special after the resurrection of Christ (Acts 20:7, Rev.1:10, Ps.118:22–24, Acts 4:10–11). There is no warrant in confusing the Sabbath (Saturday) of the Old Covenant with the "Lord's Day" (Sunday) of the New Covenant. The change in days of special worship from Saturday to Sunday parallels and symbolizes a change in covenants. Sabbath observance is linked to the Old Covenant. Sunday worship is symbolic of life under the New Covenant. As the Sabbath reflected the Old Covenant's outward conformity to a set rule of conduct so the Day of the Lord reflects an inner posture and freedom. The table below summarizes the distinction between the Old Covenant Sabbath and the New Covenant Lord's Day.

The Sabbath	*The Lord's Day*
Saturday —because of Creation	Sunday —because of Resurrection (New Creation)
A symbol of the Old Covenant	A symbol of the New Covenant
A legally fixed day	A style of life
Ex. 20	Rom. 14
For Israel	For the Church
Started with Moses	Started at Pentecost
Ended at the Cross	Continues

So How Do We Keep the Sabbath?

What does all this mean for our lives? First, it challenges our tendency to be legalistic with respect to a day of worship. Some believers will set Sunday aside as a "Sabbath day of rest." This is a great tradition to maintain, but it should not become a moral mandate that delineates the faithful from the unspiritual nor should it be a substitute for a lifestyle of "faith rest." Second, the Sabbath principle calls us to be more concerned about bringing the Sabbath to our work than working on the Sabbath. I want to approach my work with an inner peace in my soul enabling me to be productive without being spiritually stressed. Third, we cease from our striving to fulfill the law in our flesh and trust Christ. We celebrate the Sabbath aright when we walk in the radical grace of the cross. Whenever I feel shame, condemnation, or anxiety in my relationship with God, I assume I have forgotten I live under a perpetual Sabbath. Fourth, we cease from our striving to fulfill our lives in our labor and let our work become an act of worship. Radical grace is a call for the Sabbath rest for our souls. The

Sabbath rest is seen in the posture of Mary, not Martha. The Sabbath is not in opposition to work. It is a call to put work in a context that glorifies God as opposed to fulfilling our deepest needs or identity as a pseudo-Messiah.

A point to ponder

The question is not
- do you work on the Sabbath, but rather do you bring the Sabbath to your work.

Steps of Application

1. Take an inventory of your week with a journal where you record the level of anxiety and peace you experienced during the activity of each day.

2. Recall a time when you sensed you were at the feet of Jesus without the busyness of ministry. Plan to repeat the experience if you can.

3. Write a brief description of a time when you were very busy yet with the spirit of Mary.

Questions for Discussion

1. How would you summarize this chapter?

2. How have you seen Martha's posture in your life?

3. What does it mean for you to sit at Jesus feet? Is it a feeling, a mindset, or an activity? What is it?

4. How can you build safeguards into your work to make sure it is at Jesus' feet?

5. Is it a good idea to observe a special day of rest? Why? How can you turn a day of rest into a reminder of the spiritual rest that we have in Christ?

6. Are there parts of this chapter with which you disagree? Why?

Chapter 2
A Mary Spirit in a Martha World

On a sabbatical project where I visited twenty-five "successful" congregations in the West and Midwest, I observed a common struggle in nearly every congregation that I visited—finding joyful, motivated, and competent workers. When people did serve, they were too often prone to "burn out" like Martha. They lacked the joy and peace of a Mary. To make matters worse the average congregation seemed confused in addressing this problem. Living in a Martha world is challenging for a Mary. How can we equip workers with a Sabbath spirit?

Mary's spirit of worship is a vital part of Christian ministry and is expressed well in Paul's letter to the Romans. The book of Romans provides insight into the relationship between worship, sanctification, and Christian service.

Paul's Advice for Those Who Wish
To Bring the Sabbath to Their Work

Three principles mark an authentic Christian life according to Paul in Romans 12:1–8. The order of these principles is most interesting and important. First, the grace of God must be deeply sensed. We must feel secure. Second, the cross of Christ must be willingly carried. We must make sacrifices starting with our own ego. Third, the gifts of the Spirit must be properly used. We must serve. This is how Paul puts it: "*Therefore, I urge you, brothers, in view of God's mercy, to offer your bodies as living sacrifices, holy and pleasing to God—this is your spiritual act of worship. Do not conform any longer to the pattern of this world, but be transformed by the renewing of your mind. Then you will be able to test and approve what God's will is—his good, pleasing and perfect will. For by the grace given me I say to every one of you: Do not think of yourself more highly than you ought, but rather think of yourself with sober judgment, in accordance with the measure of faith God has given you. Just as each of us has one body with many members, and these members do not all have the same function, so in Christ we who are many form one body, and each member belongs to all the others. We have different gifts, according to the grace given us. If a man's gift is prophesying, let him use it in proportion to his faith. If it is serving, let him serve; if it is teaching, let him teach; if it is encouraging, let him encourage; if it is contributing to the needs of others, let him give generously; if it is leadership, let him govern diligently; if it is showing mercy, let him do it cheerfully."*

First: The Grace of God must be Deeply Sensed. We must Feel Secure.

"I urge you therefore, brethren" (Rom.12:1) is a hinge that links two great sections of Paul's letter to the Romans. The first eleven chapters of Romans deal with sitting at Jesus' feet—our wealth in Christ. The last chapters call us to ministry—our service of worship in response to grace.

Romans

Ch. 1–11	Ch. 12–16
"the mercies of God"	"our service of worship"
Sitting at Jesus' feet	Ministering to Jesus

God's people must come to deeply sense God's grace so they respond to Christ out of gratitude not duty. The first priority in Paul's view of ministry is a meaningful personal experience of God's grace. *"I urge you therefore, brethren, by the mercies of God."* Until and unless there is freedom from fear and condemnation before the law, our ministry will be improperly motivated. The warmth of God's love must be felt. Grace and love must be more than doctrines; they must encourage us to "show up" for ministry because of joy and gratitude, not duty or fear. We should respond as those who possess the very righteousness of Jesus Himself. As Paul tells us in Romans 4:5, *"But to the one who does not work, but believes in Him who justifies the ungodly, his faith is reckoned as righteousness."*

Consider the unusual position a foreign diplomat occupies in our nation's capital. Diplomats are immune from prosecution with respect to many of our laws. For example, a diplomat does not have to pay parking tickets. They are not "under the parking laws" of the District of Columbia because they are diplomats representing another nation. They are special alien ambassadors. In the same way we who have faith in Christ are alien ambassadors in this world. We too are free from the penalty of the Mosaic Law covenant. When we sin, we are not cast out or asked to pay for our sins or make atonement in order to have fellowship with God. Most diplomats obey the law out of respect for the USA and its people, not out of fear of getting a ticket. Christians also should strive to please God even though they do not "have to obey" in order to remain a part of the Christian family. This is why Paul starts chapter 12 of Romans with an appeal to obey based on the freedom and mercy we have been given in Christ. Paul does not command obedience as a *means* of justification before God nor as a notarization of justification, but rather as a *response* to justification before God.

Grace that is deeply sensed is a powerful motivator to obedience. At this point you may ask me: if radical grace is not balanced with a healthy dose of fear from the law, will not people neglect their duty to serve? Do I hear Martha calling from the kitchen? I am impressed with how well guilt, fear, and material reward work as motivators to dutiful activity. But does it have God in it? Do guilt, fear, and law produce "gold, silver, and precious stones" or "wood, hay, and straw" (1 Cor.3:10–15)?

One of my friend's six-year-old sons was playing soccer but having a rather hard time of it. After being knocked down by one of the bigger boys, he ran crying to the sidelines wanting to quit. His father tried in vain to encourage him with grace and love. The boy went over to his mother who whispered some words of motivation in his ear with the result that the lad bounded onto the field and played like a tiger. After the game the father asked his wife for the script of her secret pep talk. She said it was no secret. She simply told him, "Quitters don't get a McDonald's happy meal after the game." Knowing how to manipulate the carrot and the fear of its loss proves powerful, but is it what God wants? In our addiction to pragmatism and tangible results, we are willing to use anything that will bring "superficial" results on the field or in the kitchen. God is looking for something more than just "the right" activity especially if it is wrongly motivated.

Paul says the love (not fear) of Christ constrains him (2 Cor.5:14). We have told our children if they initiate responsibility, they will win freedom to make their own decisions. On one occasion when our sixteen year old asked how late she could stay out, we said, use your own judgment. To our pleasant surprise she came home by 10:30. When she policed herself, keeping our trust and love are the motivation. Because she does not want to lose our respect, she is extra conservative. Interestingly enough the next day she confessed she would rather we establish legalistic rules on how late she could stay out. She felt our rules would be more liberal than her self-imposed guidelines. Love and respect are the most powerful constraints.

Teaching radical grace is risky. It may free some people to neglect duties and responsibilities. But there is also a great risk in not living under grace. There are some things in our bitter souls that the law cannot tame. And we must acknowledge that what the law can tame, the flesh will use to bring glory to self. Satan has great leverage with the law. It is true that he can also distort our view of grace, but it is so much easier to use the law to make life all about ME. Paul noted that the law has jurisdiction over a person as long as he lives (Rom.7:1). It is our refusal to die with Christ that gives Satan and the law leverage to make life all about ME.

Second: The Cross of Christ must be Willingly Carried.

Sacrifices are inevitable. God's people must apply the cross to their flesh (ego) so their "ministry" is not self-serving. The radical grace of God means freedom from the terror of our sins and also freedom from the tyranny of ourselves.

The second step in Paul's priorities is found in the last part of verse 1 of Romans 12: *"Present your bodies a living and holy sacrifice."* At the cross of Christ God not only dealt with sin, He also dealt with "self." We died with Christ so as to be "born again" in the Spirit to a new sphere of living. The challenge we face is one of not only accepting our freedom from condemnation but also submitting to His rightful control of our new being. We are to see ourselves dead to our former way of thinking and acting. We are to see ourselves dead to our selfish dreams and ambitions. We are to see ourselves dead to strategies designed to protect our image. The cross takes away our sin and slays us (our old life). It then calls us to walk in forgiveness and grace and offer ourselves as a living sacrifice.

There are two kinds of self-sacrifice. One reflects a posture of personal insecurity, confused identity, and spiritual ignorance (fear, guilt, desperation) that is destructive and unwise. Another kind of self-sacrifice comes from a posture of security in Christ where we experience His grace. Paul talks about offering self as a sacrifice in chapter 12 only after chapters 1–11 where he underscores the grace of God in graphic terms. We need a full head of steam with grace before we hit 12:1–2. If we offer ourselves as a living sacrifice from a posture of shame, we are spiritually sick and need healing. When we offer ourselves as a living sacrifice in response to grace, we die to our designs and visions; we give up a demanding spirit.

Our baptism is a dramatic picture of this truth. We die to our old self and are raised to a new selfless life in Christ. We now will be called and expected to work as those who are living sacrifices. We should be careful to take our baptism seriously because we can be assured that

God will. He will call us to a life that will require personal sacrifice. When someone in our congregation is hurting, I hurt. Although admittedly sometimes my hurt is not empathetic, it is ego-related "because I could not solve their problem." My mind says, "How dare you have a problem under my teaching." When someone leaves our church, I may take it personally. But really I can't make anyone's decisions for them or manipulate them to meet my needs for acceptance and love. I have enough problems following my own advice. We must declare war on the tendency to have our ego needs met in Christian service. This will be tested as we follow Christ. The patriarch Abraham was asked to offer his only son, Isaac, back to God even though Isaac represented the key to God's promise for Abraham's future. A.W. Tozer described Abraham as a man of great wealth who possessed nothing. He had died to his own dreams and schemes and was wholly trusting in God.

> ### *A point to ponder*
>
> The service that glorifies God
> is in response to an experience
> of the grace of God.

My oldest son, Daniel, suffers from autism. When we first learned of his condition, he was eighteen months old; and we were devastated not only because we felt badly for him but because our dreams for him died. As he grew older, I realized I had to die to my expectations for him. We would never be able to play ball together or go fishing. I would not be able to communicate with him. Daniel is now in midlife and has never spoken and does not know his parents. His condition is severe and my sense of loss is great. But something very wonderful happened through my experience with "losing" my son—or my fantasy dreams for my son. His condition forced me to die to a lot of things—my selfish expectations for my other two children, my selfish dreams for my ministry, and selfish expectations for those I worked around. Ministry sacrifices can be made if we first put ourselves on the altar. And being asked to die to self seems cruel if we do not know God's love.

A point to ponder

The proof of a servant's heart is seen
in how he or she responds
when treated like one.

Whenever we offer ourselves as living sacrifices to God, we take real risks. There is no promise we will escape suffering. Ed, a radiant saint in our congregation, was asked to talk at one of our men's retreats about prayer; but we all walked away with a more powerful lesson on selflessness as we listened to his story. He told of how he prayed at his daughter's wedding that she would not be aware of the spiral fracture in his leg, knowing it would mar her special moment. As he danced (in excruciating pain) on a broken leg with his daughter, he prayed that her special moment and joy would not be diminished by knowledge of her father's personal pain. He never told her, and later as he viewed the wedding pictures and saw the smile on his face as he was photographed dancing with his daughter, he thanked God for answered prayer. We not only learned about prayer that day; we learned much more about death to self. We learned what makes Christian love and service authentic, rich, powerful, and truly fruitful.

For the Christian hope is postponed. You will be treated like a servant if you follow Jesus because God takes your death to self in baptism seriously. Be responsible but let go of ownership. Remember you will probably accomplish more by how you respond to personal injustice than by how skillfully you prevent or avoid it. What should be your first responsibility when you face failure, rejection, pain, and heartbreak? It should be to show those around you how to respond to it. Grow antenna not horns when you face rejection. You will teach more at those times by your response than by your exposition of any text on suffering. We need people who are dead to self and alive to God. We first *remember*, then we *die*, then we *serve*.

Third: The Gifts of the Spirit Must Be Properly Used.

Christians must minister primarily in the area of their giftedness. *"And since we have gifts that differ according to the grace given to us, let each exercise them accordingly"* (vs.6).

If we start talking about doing our own thing (using our gifts) before we deal with our ego, we don't have "a service of worship," we have "show time." And if we lay down our lives outside the context of God's grace, we can't call that worship. What we have in such a case is more like emotional suicide. These are typical mistakes made in our churches where we preach the use of gifts without death to self, and we preach death to self without radical grace.

The gifts of the Spirit are given to us for the edification of the church, not the edification of the gifted. At times in our lives when we are tempted to use our gift to shore up a broken childhood or a damaged self-image, we must be told to lay it down. One of the biggest challenges that we will face is the challenge to not let our service (the use of our gifts) take a messianic role in our lives. We must not let our work be the savior of *our* souls. We must not let it be the love of *our* lives. We must not let it be the source of happiness and wholeness for *our* damaged egos.

Coming to Jesus is like being invited to a banquet where he serves us as he did Mary. We come with needs for living water that only he can supply. But we come to him from a world that has conditioned us to meet our needs through our work, our merits, and our fruitfulness. Like Martha we are tempted to say, "I can't come now. I have vital work to do—work I hope will help make me okay." How many of us are using our work, relationships, ministry, or hobbies as cheap therapy? Our needs are real, but it is only at the banquet we find ourselves whole. We must follow Mary and not Martha.

Paul wrote Romans from the city of Corinth where he had an opportunity to see firsthand a negative example of the call to living sacrifice. The Corinthian church had conformed to this world even though it was very zealous for the faith. This church was focused on the Kingdom but not on the King. The Corinthians were in "Martha's kitchen" busy working for the Lord without sitting at his feet or listening to his voice. There was no sense of "dying with Christ" among the Corinthian believers. They confused style with orthodoxy when they claimed: "*I am of Paul; I am of Apollos; I am of Peter; I am of Jesus.*" They were trying to meet the needs of their souls through their leaders, through the use of their gifts, and through the demanding of their personal "spiritual" rights.

You can almost hear them complain to each other as they use their spiritual gifts to find significance—"You can't take that away from me and get away with it because you are robbing me of my feeling of wholeness." They were abusing one another with their styles of ministry. "If you are not like me, you are not worth much and certainly not following God." They were seeking selfish preferences at the expense of others. They shout, "I'm going to meet my needs; don't get in my way." You can read all about their misguided strategies in 1 Corinthians 12-14.

We are called to bear a cross to a banquet. The grace of God must be deeply sensed, the cross of Christ must be willingly carried, and the gifts of the Spirit must be rightly used. If we first sit with Mary, the work will come from the heart. We need to learn how to worship before we learn how to minister. Serving our fellowman must come in the wake of and in response to our worship of God. When we learn this, we not only find peace but also become peacemakers through our influence and example.

Steps of Application

1. Write a testimony of your life as a Martha describing all the ways you exemplify her tendencies. Note especially the pattern of Romans 12 in this chapter. Include in your testimony the ways you have not sensed God's grace, carried your cross, or used your gifts. After doing this exercise, pray over each area for God to grant you a spirit of repentance from Martha's spirit.

2. Now write a testimony of your life as a Mary, describing all the ways you exemplify her tendencies. Ask that God would "put on" this "new man" as He "puts off" the old.

3. Commit yourself to share with another person the things you have learned from this chapter.

Questions for Discussion

1. Why is Mary's posture so important to Jesus?

2. What can be done to cultivate Mary's spirit in our lives without neglecting the work of service?

3. What are the possible misunderstandings or abuses that can come from Mary's posture?

4. How would you express the message of this chapter?

5. Are there parts of this chapter with which you disagree? Why?

Chapter 3
Martha's Work Ethic

Obstacle #4 to Peace with God: Busyness Doing Good Things

We experience peace with God when we stop trying to win or keep God's favor through our behavior.

Perhaps you saw the T-shirt with the inscription, "*Jesus is coming! Look busy.*" Work has a Messianic role in the lives of too many people. It is where they look for satisfaction (security, significance, and serenity). It governs their greatest decisions, occupies most of their attention, and is the source of hope with respect to their deepest longings. It is where they offer most of their sacrifices.

We looked at three obstacles to peace in my previous book *Peace Seekers*. The foolish builder taught us to sabotage peace by ignoring holiness. Hagar taught us we sabotage peace in our lives by living under the law. Satan sabotages peace by convincing us to put faith in anything and everything but Christ. Martha will teach us we can sabotage peace by being busy—even busy doing the Lord's work. A fourth obstacle to peace is busyness. A busy soul has a hard time making peace.

But Don't we Need a Lot More Marthas?

Garrison Keillor, quoted in *U.S. Catholic* magazine, said: "I'm not so sure I'm in favor of repentance. Sinners are the ones who get the work done. A strong sense of personal guilt is what makes people willing to serve on committees." There is no doubt that guilt and fear are powerful motivators, but does good work done apart from a spirit of worship really glorify God? I believe that Jesus would have been disappointed if Martha's work was left undone. It was not Martha's work but the way she viewed her work that was the issue?

I have so often heard the protest: "But if we don't do the work, who will?" "If we don't fret and worry, it won't get done." "If we don't push and pull, no one will move." Like Martha we might feel drawn into the kitchen of activity. We might share her impatience with those who seem oblivious to the vast responsibilities that face the Christian in her family, church, community, job, and world. But God may need to call some of us out of the kitchen until we learn to bring worship to our work.

The word on the street is we are a generation of spectators, consumers, and critics who have time for everything but God's work. It seems we need a lot more Marthas. There is a shrinking volunteer pool for the "Martha's kitchen chores" in the average church. We are told what we need is a deeper sense of duty; a little guilt might be appropriate in recruiting hands to make the work lighter.

In doing research for a previous book, *Put Your Best Foot Forward* (Abingdon), I visited twenty-five of the "most respected" congregations in this country. My findings revealed certain common characteristics. First, they have a shortage of quality volunteers for the children's programs. Recruiting lay ministers is a year-round task in most churches. Second, they also have a shortage of middle level lay leaders for ministries. Some people are willing to carry out an assignment, but few lay leaders are available to divvy out assignments and take responsibility to make sure the job gets done right. Getting and keeping mature small group leaders is the weak link in many congregations. As one pastor told me, "As soon as we get a person trained, it seems they burn out or get transferred to a different community through their work." The story of Mary and Martha cannot sit well with the obsessive-compulsive, type-A workaholic for the Lord. There is no doubt we need laborers in the kitchen of ministry, but do the folks in the kitchen minister as an expression of worship, or is it just work duty? At the end of the shift is God being glorified and the Kingdom being demonstrated? Or are we just trying to look good while we burn out?

Am I a Martha?

How many of the following statements describe your lifestyle?

1. I am a perfectionist about my work.

2. I look like I am confident and at peace, but I really am insecure and anxious.

3. I set difficult goals and unrealistic expectations for others and myself making myself vulnerable to feelings of guilt and bitterness.

4. When things don't go as I expect, I tend to get irritable and angry.

5. I worry a lot about meeting my responsibilities.

6. I feel responsible for too much.

7. I think of myself as someone who works hard and plays hard.

8. I tend to define the Christian life in terms of duties.

9. I find it very hard to meditate and worship when there are tasks that need to be done.

10. I have a hard time saying no when people call on me to serve.

11. I feel the greatest need in my life is more self-discipline.

12. I have an especially hard time with people who are heavenly minded but no earthly good.

13. I tend to feel guilty when I am not working.

14. I find it hard to relax, have fun, and play without feeling guilty.

If you find yourself identifying with any of these statements, you may have a Martha spirit on board. There are many responsibilities that face anyone claiming to follow Jesus, but the most important is listening at His feet. Two things characterize Disciples of Christ: 1) they see things through Christ's eyes and 2) they hear things through Christ's Spirit. Before we venture into the field to work, we need to learn how to listen and see life from a posture of worship. The Martha spirit will find the challenge of worship uncomfortable, irritating, or more often foreign. Martha's problem was not that she was serving, but rather that she was serving without the renewed mind of a worshipper.

A point to ponder

Too many of us worship at work,
work at play,
and play at worship.

When Martha Dresses like Mary

Martha can take Mary's posture at the feet of Jesus and still be the Martha of the kitchen. Marthas tend to turn everything and anything into a duty of obligation. We have all heard the phrase, "Are we having fun yet?" Well, how about the phrase, "Are we worshipping yet?" It is possible to be obsessive-compulsive with worship. A Martha attitude wants to be sure she is doing it just right and that everyone else is too.

I attended an ecumenical Easter service some time ago involving a number of different Christian traditions. After the service one of the pastors shared with me his discomfort with the fact that the congregation did not really enter into worship. The people kept praising and singing, but they really weren't worshipping by his definition. When I asked him how he could tell if someone was worshipping or not, he told me he could sense the Spirit of God in the body language of the congregation. When they started moving with passion and joy, they were apparently "in the Spirit." Until then they were just going through the motions. I had never really considered that there were worship police who would spend their time making sure that worship was done right, but that's because I didn't expect to find Martha dressed up like Mary.

A Lutheran pastor told me the story of a church service where a visitor raised her hands in the middle of the worship service and exclaimed in a loud voice, "Praise the Lord!" An established member of the congregation tapped her on the shoulder and quietly said, "We don't "praise the Lord" in this congregation." Her husband corrected her saying, "Yes we do, dear. It is on page 41 of the hymnal." Much of our worship simply follows the tradition we are comfortable with not realizing that the language and style is not the issue from God's point of view. But going through the motions of our liturgies be they disciplined ritual or spontaneous emotion mean nothing if they do not convey a respectful heart of awe and thankfulness—seeing and listening at Jesus' feet.

The writings of Thomas Merton, a Trappist Monk, have made an impression on my life. Merton draws attention to the temptation within us to rush to work for God without knowing Him or having intimate fellowship with Him. Such work though "fruitful" in the eyes of others lacks "shalom" (peace), which I believe is a distinctive characteristic marking the true fruit of God's Spirit. Anxiety, weariness of spirit, and a nagging sense of never having done enough will mark the life of one who works obediently for God without experiencing God working through him or her. We must always strive to know God and not just obey Him. Christianity is distinct from Judaism and Islam at this point. While all three religions stress obedience, both Judaism and Islam do not stress knowing God in the intimate way Christ prescribes. Christian work, no matter how faithful, is not a substitute for a deep, intimate experience of God and His love. Such knowledge is not always easy to come by, but as it comes, it will bring peace with it. When ministry work is engaged from this posture of worship, it will have God in it.

Christians live under four mandates. Each of these mandates calls for acts of obedience that should be motivated by a sense of worship, but too often they are motivated only by duty. These mandates represent venues of responsibility exciting the Martha within us. There are many opportunities for a "Martha spirit" to stay in the kitchen and work up a sweat over any or all of these responsibilities. Can we meet the challenge of being responsible to each of them while sitting at Jesus' feet?

A point to ponder

Just because people are working hard to serve Christ does not mean God is working though them or that they should expect peace.

The Cultural Mandate

In Genesis 2 humans are called to subdue the earth and have dominion over creation. This calling has been known as "the cultural mandate" in that it places an obligation on God's people to take care of their natural environment, including the general culture. While we should take this mandate seriously, I am surprised that it does not seem to receive a lot of attention in the writings of the apostles or the teachings of Jesus. There are three places however where care for the general culture appears in the writings of the New Testament. First, this mandate includes doing good to all mankind. Paul exhorts us in Galatians 6:10 to *"do good to all men, especially to those who believe."* In this text we have a clear call to live our lives to benefit all people whether or not they share our faith. Second, Jesus teaches His disciples to *"render unto Caesar the things that are Caesar's and unto God the things that are God's"* (Matt. 22:21). In the USA this means we vote, lend our voice to the public square, live virtuous civic lives, and generally respect the common good and civil government. Third, this cultural mandate also calls for commitment to family. Paul tells us: if we do not care for the members of our own family, we are worse than those who do not believe (1 Tim.5:8). Perhaps the greatest contribution we make in our generation to the welfare of the broader culture is in our commitment to supporting the family. This may prove to be more important than the goods and services we provide in our vocations.

How does grace relate to the cultural mandate? Grace should be woven into our actions, not separate from them. First, we must recognize that the cultural mandate—our vocational commitments and family commitments—constitute a great challenge. The challenge is not that we will be unengaged but rather that we will be engaged in the right way. As I have suggested earlier, vocation and family can take on a messianic role—becoming the objects of our sacrificial worship, governing our life decisions, and providing the greatest comfort and reward to our lives. If we live under radical grace, we will be free from an unholy and unhealthy attachment to our work, nation, and families.

Second, we must bring our Sabbath rest to our work. The question is not do we work on the Sabbath, but rather do we bring the Sabbath to our work. Can we relate to our world with a relaxed inner attitude, or are we driven by anxiety and a sense of burden? Joy, peace, and freedom are our signatures of grace. This is our salt and light to the world. If we reflect the fear, anger, guilt, and despair of our culture, how can we expect the world to listen when we speak of the peace of the gospel? Grace puts us at rest with our environment, our fellow man, and ourselves because we are at rest with God. Peacemaking flows from a heart that works hard but also works in the spirit of the Sabbath.

The third way in which grace and our cultural mandate intersect is through the recognition that we have four mandates that deserve respect. Our responsibility is not only centered on building or conserving culture. As a matter of fact the cultural mandate receives less direct attention in Scripture than do the other three callings. Grace does not produce anxiety about having to do everything. It lives peacefully with the knowledge that the "Body of Christ" has many members with different roles. Many of our misplaced priorities come from failing to see the bigger picture of what God is doing apart from us. Our individual passions, gifts, opportunities, and place in life should dictate the degree to which we are involved in making the cultural mandate a central part of our personal agenda.

> ### A point to ponder
>
> **It is not about how much we produce but rather about who we become.**

The Commission Mandate

In Matthew 28:19–20 Jesus commissions His followers to make disciples of all nations. The Apostle Paul reiterates this mandate in Ephesians 4 where he places emphasis on building up the body of Christ by the proper working of every part. In Paul's view the object of Jesus' commission was the spiritual formation and maturation of the Body of Christ—the church. Evangelism was only the first step in bringing people to spiritual maturity. In this context grace is central to the building process as we unify the Body of Christ (peacemaking) through love (Eph.4:11-16).

Earlier in my Christian walk I was exhorted to share my faith with those who had not received Christ as their Lord and Savior. This exhortation came with a fair amount of Scripture quoting and guilt as a motivation. But at the time I had experienced little of Christ's life, and I had not yet learned the importance of worship. My attempts at sharing my faith were not only awkward and burdensome but also ineffective and selfish. I was doing it to be accepted by my spiritual handlers, not because I loved God or the people who needed to hear the gospel. We pay a price when we put work before worship even when that work is "God's work." Exhortation to ministry is needed and certainly consistent with the biblical text, but we must exhort as Paul did—appealing to our identity in Christ and responding to His grace. Exhortation needs a gracious context if it is to be of the Spirit of Christ and effective.

But in a production oriented culture the church can be too focused on Martha's kitchen. One of the intriguing tools of the modern church has been the expanding use of sociology and secular management techniques in ministry. Because "it works," it attracts the attention of many gifted leaders who may tend to struggle with Martha's spirit. If these leaders are not careful, they can find the glitter of Martha's high-tech kitchen irresistible. Mary's way may be too slow, too inactive, and too reflective to cash in on the "advantages" of the new toys (spiritual kitchen appliances) for church growth and social reclamation.

The staff of large congregations must be committed to modeling principles of gracious relationships which include: 1) a freedom to fail in striving to reach goals, 2) a commitment to supporting an individual's well-being, even if it means sacrificing productive efficiency, and 3) an integrity in relationships with respect to honesty, deference, sensitivity, and humility. We want to model *joy* in ministry, not a frantic obsession to reach productivity goals or a desperate urgency in our responsibility for ministry.

Have you noticed how inefficient and "unproductive" (by our standards) Jesus and the Apostles seemed to be? Jesus only ministered for three short years. Paul spent more time in prison than on mission trips. I am constantly reminded of Jesus' lack of frantic activity in contrast to our anxious lifestyles. Didn't Jesus realize the whole world was on its way to hell? How could he not spend every waking hour spreading the Gospel? There was no time to waste in meditation, reflection, prayer, etc. Now was the time to act. We do need evangelists but from the house of Mary not from Martha's kitchen.

I am of the belief that if the staff of a church can model for the congregation lives of peace with healthy gracious relationships, then they can with power exhort the fellowship toward the same kind of behavior. The discipleship mandate is a very big part of our calling and deserves center stage. Jesus' Spirit is in the business of making disciples that have the same style of life we see in Jesus and his Apostles. It is a style of faith, hope, and love that is contagious and makes peace. We are to make disciples of Christ not disciples of a Christian subculture that too often reflect western values—materialism, pragmatism, individual rights, etc. These virtues do not easily lend themselves to peace or peacemaking.

The Charismatic Mandate

In Romans 12:1–8 Paul calls Christians to *use their gifts or* special talents to build up the church. We will have different roles in the body of Christ. Those differences should be related to our unique gifts. There is a mandate from God that we respect, develop, and use our own giftedness and that we honor the giftedness of others.

Let us go back again to the sequence in Paul's argument in Romans 12 (previous chapter). He starts with God's grace toward us. He then calls for self-sacrifice. And only then does he exhort us with respect to the proper use of our gifts. In short gifts that are used without first sacrificing personal needs for security and significance will probably wind up being used to achieve personal security and significance. These needs are to be met by Christ not our ministry. Healthy self-sacrifice will not take place without a deep sense of God's love and grace. I minister with integrity when I do so without needing to have my own pain medicated, identity established, or ego padded through ministering. Finding, developing, and implementing our "spiritual gifts" can become another obsession for the Martha spirit in us. This is especially true if we fail to understand and embrace the order of Romans 12 as expressed in the previous chapter. Peacemakers must know how to celebrate diversity of roles in the Body of Christ lest they marginalize the importance of another's calling or refuse to respect the boundaries of their own.

The Character Mandate

As if the Martha in us did not have enough to do, let's not forget we need to perfect our character. In Colossians 3:1–17 and elsewhere Paul calls us to personal godliness, to maturity of character. We are called to live lives consistent with our new identity in Christ, and there are few challenges met with more anxiety and frustration. Who among us has not felt at one time or another they should be more together by this point in their lives? The growing market for self-help books suggest there is no lack of motivation for personal change, but are we running the race toward "maturity in Christ" without grace? Having begun in the Spirit are we being perfected in the flesh (Gal.3:3). The goal of godliness is best achieved in the context of radical acceptance, not fear of rejection. Therapists have learned that unless a person feels safe, accepted, and understood, he or she will probably not change. We are being transformed by grace to grace. We love because He first loved us. We forgive because we have been forgiven. Our service is a response not just to needs that we see but to grace that we have experienced. Jesus told his disciples to bear fruit by "abiding in him" rather than focus on producing the fruit. They need to follow Mary's example. Martha's spirit does not lend itself to peacemaking.

True Virtue is a "Mary Thing."

There are many lists in the New Testament that describe what God expects of his people. I do not know of any list that includes a word about being busy or even productive.

It is usually about character qualities. It is as though the issue is not how much we produce but rather who we become. As we face each of these mandates, we are challenged not only to "do" but also to "be." We are to bring a sense of worship to our work. We are to live lives that are not only productive but also peaceful.

Steps of Application

1. As you reflect on your answers to the inventory early in this chapter, what do you conclude about your soul's posture?

2. Take a moment to reflect on your activity as a Christian and note at which moments you experience joy, peace, and a sense of gratitude.

3. Of the four ministry mandates mentioned in this chapter, which gets the most attention in your life? Do you sense there is need for more balance?

4. Take a number of life decisions you have made recently and subject them to the fourfold callings at the end of this chapter.

Questions for Discussion

1. How can we correct the Martha impulse in our culture and lives?

2. Should you put all work on hold until you develop a worship attitude?

3. Do you know anyone around you that models a proper spirit at work? What is it that impresses you about their lives?

4. How can you encourage those around you to put worship in their work?

5. Are there parts of this chapter with which you disagree? Why?

Chapter 4
Things Heat Up in the Kitchen

Martha's middle name is stress.

Ann and her husband Ben (not their real names) were going through major stress in their marriage. This was Ann's second marriage and Ben's third. Ann was seriously considering ending this relationship that seemed to bring to her life more stress than satisfaction. She was stressed at a new job where she was managing a number of challenging subordinates. She had health problems that could be serious. On top of all this she was not feeling that Ben was sensitive to her anxiety and was not doing enough to protect her from the circumstances that were overwhelming her especially from his children by a former marriage who were never in favor of this marriage.

Ann's story illustrates a very common situation. Stress is our experience when we as imperfect people bring unrealistic expectations into an imperfect world. As a Christian Ann had been baptized into Christ, and the Spirit of Christ had been installed in the core (holy of holies) of her life. But like so many of us she had given a lot of other things access to the control center of her life expecting these things to have messianic roles in her story. She personalized the rejection of her in-laws giving them authority to grade her soul's value. She brought to her work an expectation of others and herself that would define her significance as a person. Her health problems just seemed to aggravate her attempts to manage her other difficult circumstances. As is often the case when we are stressed and cannot change our circumstances, we turn to those around us for protection from the world. Ann expected her husband to relieve the pain which he could not. This looks a lot like Martha's anger toward Mary. Could Mary have relieved Martha's stress by leaving Jesus to help her? Yes, but this would not really address Martha's core issues.

What we need to understand is that there are two paths we can take to find peace in this scenario. We can find a way to change our outer circumstances, or we can renew our mind to process the circumstances in a different way. The first strategy just kicks the issue down the road since sooner or later we, as imperfect people, will again face an imperfect world. When Jesus invited his disciples to be equally yoked with him in life, they were told that the load would be light. Jesus was speaking of the emotional / psychological effect of reserving the holy of holies (control room) in the disciple's soul to be his exclusive domain. In the above case Ann needed to 1) stop trying to manage her stress by manipulating her outward circumstances, and 2) give attention to kicking out the crowd she had amassed in her holy of holies who were convincing her to find her security, significance, and serenity in all the wrong places. 3) refrain from making things worse by pressuring her husband to change the imperfect world that she could not. The words of Jeremiah come back to us: *"For My people have committed two evils: they have forsaken Me, the fountain of living waters, to hew for themselves cisterns, broken cisterns that can hold no water."* (2:13) Martha and Mary provide an opportunity to make this same point. We might represent Ann's situation with the following chart.

The origin of Toxic Stress

Imperfect people   +   *Imperfect world*

Distorted Expectations meet Disappointing Experiences

Two Responses

Change the world	*Change the perspective*
Manipulate the environment.	**Renew the mind.**
Get protection from others.	**Reinstall Jesus as Messiah**

Why do people seek pastoral counseling? There are of course many presenting reasons but most can be traced back to a lack of personal happiness—feeling stressed and eventually depressed. When people are at peace, they are generally happy; and they do not seek help from others. Unhappiness is almost always stress related—inner anger, fear of the future, threatening circumstances, etc.

In his book, *Thrive*, National Geographic explorer Dan Buettner seeks out some of the happiest people in the world (living in the "Blue Zones") to learn their secret. Denmark ranked top on the list as the country with the happiest citizens. When the Danes were asked why they were happy, they typically responded, "We face little stress. It is true we pay high taxes, but we are one of the wealthiest nations per capita in the world. We have lifelong health care. Education is free. We trust our leaders and there is not a great gap between the wealthy and the poor." Americans do not rank high on the list of happiest people. Part of this may be related to the byproducts of individual freedom. In Singapore (ranked #2 among happiest countries) there is no free press, one political party rules, and people are punished harshly for "minor" social infractions. How can this breed happiness? One young Singaporean mother responded, "The idea that American democracy is the only path to freedom is arrogant. I'd rather live in a place where it's safe for my kids to play today than one where I can read *Playboy* tomorrow?" Stress is a major characteristic of our modern free society, and some of it can be healthy; but do we pay too high a price for our insistence of personal freedom? A micromanaging boss, health problems, children at risk, and a struggle to make financial ends meet…sometimes it can feel like the burdens of the world are on your shoulders. Martha was consumed with frustration and stress—so much to do and a sister that seemed disengaged with the task at hand. But as Jesus pointed out, Mary was not the problem? The true nature of stress comes not so much from the circumstances that we face but from the inner posture of our souls in facing those circumstances.

If I were the apostle Paul, and knew I was called by God to bring the gospel to the whole Gentile world and then was put out of circulation in prison, I would be frustrated, angry, and stressed to say the least. In writing Philippians from prison Paul gave little indication of stress. Why? The inner posture of his soul enabled him to respond to his dire circumstances with a remarkable peace. Paul's personal significance and security were established through an experience of God's radical grace, a grace that freed him to flex with the circumstances, retain his joy, use his creativity, keep his focus, and selflessly obey God. He could see beyond his circumstances and hear something louder than the moans of his human fears and confusion. This should be our goal.

If there is a character quality that should mark the Christian as distinct in modern American culture, it might be inner peace, which issues in outer graciousness. There should be a sense of rest within the soul that the world can't give, take away, or easily explain. The ebb and flow of difficult circumstances provide a wonderful opportunity to showcase God's grace and peace. The apostle Paul writing to the Philippians of his joy while imprisoned models this spiritual peace and the peacemaking it produces.

Shalom of the Heart

The Bible uses the Hebrew word *shalom*, which is often translated "peace." It conveys the idea of being blessed inwardly and outwardly. It means being reconciled with God, neighbor, and self. It is the state of being that can best be described by Paul's salutation, "grace and peace."

How would you feel if you were living on a tight budget and received two unexpected letters—the first from the IRS telling you that you owed $2,000 in back taxes, and the second informing you that you had just inherited $200,000 from a deceased relative. Would the second letter change your initial stress level created by the first letter? It probably would leave you feeling rather carefree and joyful. Why? After all, the content of the first letter had not changed. You still owed $2,000 but now it was not such a threatening debt. The critical issue in determining your peace was not the external circumstance so much as the broader context through which you viewed it—in this case the anticipation of what it would cost you in terms of pain. It is not the content but the *context* of our circumstances that determines our level of peace.

When our oldest son, who suffers from autism, was living at home, my wife and I experienced tremendous stress. By the time he reached his eighth birthday, he had become very difficult to manage. We took two-hour shifts with Daniel because someone had to be with him all the time to keep him from crawling through a window, hurting himself, or destroying the house. When I ask myself why this challenge was stressful, I don't focus on Daniel but on the inner goal structure of my life. Daniel presented a demand on me that was not difficult to meet so long as my life was focused on meeting his needs. But my life was focused on other issues like ministry to my congregation, care for my marriage and other children, personal hobbies, and time with friends. These other aspects of life gave meaning and a sense of significance to my soul. Daniel was starving me of my soul's food, as he demanded more and more time. This inner goal structure of my soul was the cause of the stress. If I could not restructure my inner life's goals and values, I would not be able to change the stress level and behavior. The stress would not be relieved until I found a way to sense the peace of God in my soul through an experience of God's radical grace and love freeing me from having to have life experiences that authenticated me. To be sure there would also be a need to change priorities, manage competing responsibilities, and adjust my expectations of others and myself. I would also need to make creative decisions to work out the best situation for the whole family not just for Daniel.

A note of warning is in order here. It is possible to gain a certain sense of "temporal" peace by altering our circumstances while never challenging our "self-serving" goals. In my own life example I could have relieved my stress with respect to my son's care by selfishly deserting my family and starting a new life for myself somewhere else. I could also find peace by having Daniel's care centered outside our home. Each of these actions would bring a measure of temporary peace but would not address the real spiritual issue of my soul's goal structure. Can you see why it is dangerous to let "peace" be the primary guide to identify God's will for one's life? Peace can too often be fueled by idolatrous goals and self-protective strategies. True spiritual peace can indeed be a good indication we are on the right road, but can we always tell the difference between spiritual and fleshly peace? Let me offer some indicators of true peace.

Signs of True Peace

The first sign that our peace is of God and not something else is revealed in our response when threatening circumstances come. Peace is present when we retain what I call the five "C"s—contentment, courage, creativity, caring, and cooperation. If our peace is a manifestation of the flesh, we will too often respond to stress with a defensive posture, withdrawal from others, and a lack of energy to solve the problem. Or we will pass the blame onto someone or something else. Outside stressors should not rob us of contentment (the sense that all is well with our soul), courage (energy to move ahead), creativity (the ability to address difficult problems in innovative and constructive ways), caring (putting the needs of others before ourselves), or cooperation (the willingness to embrace others in a sense of community and not turn on them in frustration).

A second sign of true peace will be seen in our "attitude" when our sacred cows are threatened. A sacred cow is like the golden calf the Israelites worshiped in the wilderness. God had instructed the Israelites when leaving Egypt to take the gold and silver of the Egyptians with them as they crossed the Red Sea (Ex.3:21-22). It was that gift of God that later would become an idol of worship (Ex.32:23-24). A sacred cow is a domestic animal, something that has a good purpose but can become an idol when misused. Just about anything can become a sacred cow—people, hobbies, ministry, etc. Sacred cows are hard to identify when you are riding them or feeding them. We recognize them most often when they are taken away, and we go berserk. If you decide to hunt down the sacred cows of your life to shoot them, you will find they are easier to hit than they are to kill. They tend to be stubborn and not stay down long. This is the point. Godly peace has the power to graciously adjust when our crutches, painkillers, security blankets, and other sacred cows are taken away. We know we have peace when we lose our "sacred cows" and are not consumed with anger or anxiety but are able to move on with life. Traumatic anger and crippling fear at the loss of worldly crutches are good indicators that the peace I thought I had was not of God.

The third sign of godly peace is consistency. Circumstances change but godly peace does not take its cues from outer circumstances. True peace will not pass away with the changing of our lot in life. This is not to suggest that those who have true peace will never be challenged or anxious. The peace of God will however mark the general countenance of a person's life with a sense of rest and confidence.

Some of us spend too much of our time and energy trying to find a medication for our souls because of a lack of spiritual peace. We mask the pain and anxiety with busyness, or we use the busyness to try to find rest for our souls. We do the Martha thing—using busyness as a salve on the spiritual wounds in our lives. To make matters worse, we are encouraged by our churches and society to keep up the busyness because it appears to be productive. Here is a test to identify your level of spiritual peace. Can you meet the demands of any circumstance you might face with love, joy, and a relaxed attitude? Can you have your preferences interrupted by the unexpected demands of life's "high inside fast pitch" and still function with grace? Most of us are not there yet, but that is where we should strive to be. That is what grace and peace look like when they are installed in our lives. Furthermore as we experience and express this peace, we become peacemakers. This kind of peace is contagious.

The Peace Process

We would like to find peace instantly, but that is seldom our experience. More often than not finding peace is a process that takes time and patience. The tendency of the Martha within us is to look at peace as a goal achieved through hard work. Marthas tend to feel guilty because they don't have peace and seek it through working harder lest they experience shame. The peace process requires time and grace. Marthas must get their eyes off false peace and onto Christ and his grace.

Our motives and goal structures are complex and not easily identified or changed. We learn our strategies for dealing with life from our parents, our culture, and our unique experiences growing up in a fallen world. Martha's spirit is deeply ingrained in many of us and is not easily dislodged. There were some things I learned from early life experience that I have had to challenge. Early on in life I got the idea that assertiveness was equated with pride, which was not to be tolerated. Interestingly enough I also learned to be very proud but keep it hidden. To this strange combination of twisted virtues was added a strong work ethic. It made little difference whether my work was productive or wisely directed; what mattered was the effort. Hard work, false humility, and social passivity were supposed to give significance to my soul. This is a prescription for neurosis…or at least an ulcer. I could not deal with these "demons" until I identified them as such. And even then it would take time and discipline to keep them at bay, let alone lay them to rest.

Where Work and Peace Meet

Four things have helped me find peace in the midst of work. First, I had to recognize that the "relaxed inner attitude" of my soul was a high priority to God. Romans 14:17–19 reads, *"For the kingdom of God is not eating and drinking, but righteousness and peace and joy in the Holy Spirit. For he who in this way serves Christ is acceptable to God and approved by men. So then let us pursue the things which make for peace and the building up of one another."* Peace with my neighbor starts with peace with myself. Too often I was willing to sacrifice peace for appearances of productivity. I applauded the Marthas around me for "hard work" and "getting the job done." The message I sent to those around me was, "At all cost do what you have to do to be productive, efficient, or at least hard working. It's great if you can be productive without being anxious. But if you live a life of anxiety in the process of getting the job done, don't worry about it."

The one criticism I didn't want to hear was that I was lazy, irresponsible, or unproductive. My significance was usually defined by my outward productivity. This is the Martha syndrome. If I were to find peace for my soul, rest in my work, and joy in my trials; I would have to be willing to critically reassess my strategies in living. I would have to be willing to make peace a virtue worthy of sacrifice. I would have to see my witness to the world defined in terms of inner peace more than outward productivity. I would have to learn that peace was a high priority. If I did not have peace, I would create anxiety and anger in those around me. I would not be a peacemaker.

The second piece of advice I would give to those who want to escape the Martha syndrome is this, replace busyness with quiet time. By quiet time I don't only mean reading the Bible, meditating, and praying on a regular basis. I also suggest we cultivate a gentle and quiet inner spirit that we take with us to our work. The peace of God is not a peace or rest devoid of activity. A person can work very hard and long hours and still display this peace of soul. By the same token a person can spend all their time in meditative activity and have no peace at all. The people that display the kind of peace I desire are generally hard working and productive. Their work possesses eternal value because they live for something higher than their work.

I have a friend who for several years was a professor of political science at UNC Chapel Hill. This professor is not a Christian, but he had a very committed Christian from our congregation as a graduate student. On one occasion when this professor and I were walking together across campus, he mentioned how impressed he was with this Christian student. Unlike the other graduate students who were consumed with anxiety and afraid to say or do anything that would jeopardize their academic success, this student was fearless. This student shared his creative ideas freely. He seemed to have little concern about protecting his image in the department or securing a treasured position after graduation. As a result of his freedom, this young student was able to produce some of the best work in his department. The professor told me, "I would like to have all my graduate students know that freedom." Later as I talked with this student, he shared with me the simple reality that he was not that concerned about his graduate program. As a matter-of-fact he said he had often considered dropping out. What really mattered to him was his Christian faith and witness. He found personal significance in his union with Christ not his academic success. This young student is now himself a professor at a leading Christian university where he is not only teaching political science but also modeling a Christian lifestyle of worship. He is a peacemaker.

The third word of advice is use the Sabbath tradition of one day of rest in six to break away from old patterns. In chapter one we addressed the Sabbath issue more fully, but let me again encourage you to observe the Sabbath as a tutorial in resting from the worry and busyness of life. Make it a day where you meditate without worrying, worship without ministering to others, and rest without planning your work. A good technique to get started might include the following discipline. Designate a "worry box" in your favorite room. On the morning of your Sabbath imagine all of your concerns being put in that box for storage during the Sabbath. At the end of the Sabbath period you can go back and pick them up again if you wish, but for the Sabbath they are in storage. Then go on and live the Sabbath day as though you had no worry. With a little practice you might find a wonderful peace awaiting you so that a perpetual Sabbath becomes your lifestyle.

Lastly, be careful what you are teaching those around you especially your kids. Teach them how to live a life of peace. This is best done not by lectures but by modeling it before them. Let them see Mary in you more than Martha. Martha's frustration with Mary is too often our frustration with the Mary in us and around us. We value the Martha over the Mary in us. Don't make that mistake. Be a peacemaker–starting at home.

Legalism Confuses Caring with Controlling.

Legalism is a common tendency with the Marthas of the world. As Christians we are called to be the keeper of our brothers and sisters. That is to say we are to care for the well being of God's family. Martha's spirit tends to push this calling to a point where too much responsibility is assumed for others. This intrusive sense of over-responsibility is often coupled with a projection of the legalist's personal preferences and values onto others as moral mandates. Legalism is the improper use of the law. It is the failure to use the law lawfully. Usually it involves an emphasis on rules about relatively minor issues. It also suggests there are significant consequences to our acceptance based on performance. Legalism is the absence of radical grace. In Corinth and Galatia issues of legalism were addressed with a kind of harshness that suggests this misuse of the law is not a minor issue. It is common to confuse caring with controlling.

I met a Christian teacher when I was a university student who told me I could not simultaneously have a credit card and be obedient to Christ. This man's assumption was that everyone would face the same temptations with a credit card he faced. For him the credit card was a threat, but that was not my experience. He added that because so many people struggled to control the use of credit cards, it was unwise to set an example that would encourage others to use a card they might not be able to handle. While his point is well taken, *he* can't make the call for *me*. I must make that call freely without the intimidation of a threat of rejection or condemnation from him or anyone else. Legalism is the projection of my personal application of Biblical principles on others. Some Christians believe association with certain political philosophies or parties (liberal or conservative) cannot be reconciled with orthodox faith. This kind of legalism represents a very simplistic view of ethics that, in my judgment, cannot be justified. We all have a tendency to project onto others our personal experiences and preferences as moral law. This is legalism. Martha's spirit creates stress for Martha and those around her as she projects her own private strategies and priorities for life onto others. In doing so she is not a peacemaker.

If you are Not a Martha, you may have to Endure the Scorn of One.

One of the prices we pay when we leave Martha's kitchen to join Mary at Jesus' feet is criticism. As I indicated I was raised in a culture where the unforgivable sin was laziness. You could be forgiven for stealing, lying, and murder; but it was common knowledge in the Midwest farm country where I grew up that neither God nor man would tolerate laziness. Two quotes I remember being thrown around in the culture of my youth were, "God helps those who help themselves," and "Some people are so heavenly minded, they are no earthly good." My culture loved the Martha types, and we knew how to level scorn at those who, for whatever reason, were not working hard enough.

Don't misunderstand me. I am not arguing against hard work. I happen to think that too often we can excuse our irresponsibility with a shallow piety. We may deserve criticism if we are truly lazy and refuse to work. Remember Martha's problem was not that she was serving Jesus in tangible ways, but rather that she was doing so with little experience of His grace and peace. The question is sometimes asked, "Isn't it necessary to do the right thing for the wrong reason sometimes?" It is certainly better than doing the wrong thing for the wrong reason. But I must resist the temptation to listen to the Marthas around me who don't care why I am doing the work just so long as I do it. Disciples of Jesus listen to God's Spirit not the spirit of a culture dominated by the Martha spirit.

I recall a frantic request from a concerned woman in our congregation. She wanted me to do something about an impending financial shortfall with respect to our annual budget. Her words were, "You are just like my husband; you never worry. Well somebody better worry because if they don't, things will fall apart." I asked her, "And what will happen if they fall apart?" "Well," she replied, "I can see you just don't seem to care." For Martha, caring and worrying were synonymous. For too many people caring means controlling, worrying, manipulating, fearing, and working around the clock. I cannot recall a time when Jesus was in a hurry, and yet he only had a ministry of three years with no air travel, personal computer, or agent. And Paul said Jesus came in the "fullness of time." Will God get the job done without our fretting? I think so.

When we are pressured to be busy at the expense of worship, or when we are pushed to work beyond our level of faith; we must be willing to ask ourselves and others some hard questions: Am I doing this for me, for you, or for God? Am I willing to stop and listen before I fly into the next task? Is God in my work? Am I a worshipper at my work, or am I burning out? I don't want to rust out or burn out. I want to finish the race with the joy of the run spread across my face.

It is this impulse to work that not only marks us as those who bear the image of God, but it also can become a part of our greatest temptation—to be God or at least control our world as though we were God.

Steps of Application

1. Run through the Martha checklist in chapter three once again. Is there an area that you can change?

2. Make an honest list of the motivating reasons behind the last disappointing work experience you had. What does this tell you about your identification with Martha?

3. The first step to getting out of Martha's kitchen is to recognize there is no virtue in being there. Are you willing to pay the price by not doing everything others might expect of you? If you follow Mary, you may have to endure the criticism of Martha.

4. Set aside a time each day to give thanks to God and turn the events of the day over to Him.

Questions for Discussion

1. What are some early signs of a Martha spirit?

2. What is the strongest argument that can be made in favor of Martha's posture?

3. How do you plan to handle the scorn of the Marthas in your life?

4. Is it possible for Martha to have Mary's spirit and still do the kitchen work? How would the different spirit look and feel in the kitchen?

5. How would you summarize this chapter?

6. Are there parts of this chapter with which you disagree? Why?

Section II

Grace and Repentance

The Story of Two Brothers: The Prodigal and the Older Brother

The path to grace is not moral merit and discipline but brokenness and repentance.

"Men do not differ much about what things they call evils; they differ enormously about what evils they will call excusable." *G. K. Chesterton*

"People do not mind their faults being spread out before them, but they become impatient if called on to give them up." *Goethe*

Radical grace calls for radical repentance. In order to understand what that means we turn our attention to one of Jesus' greatest stories. The parable of the prodigal son is a story of three people—the prodigal, his older brother, and their father. Its spiritual message is a tale of brokenness, pride, and grace. In this section we are going to focus attention on the subject of repentance. What does it mean and how does it come about? We will see that in our relationship with God, our obedience to the law is not as important as our brokenness before it. God resists the proud and gives grace to the humble. We will follow the pilgrimage of the prodigal from his rebellion to his restoration by grace. We will see that the repentance of the son was more than just recognizing and turning from the self-indulgence of his activity in the distant land. It involved leaving the distant land and coming home. Repentance for the prodigal son included changing his physical and spiritual address with a new frame of reference and a new sense of identity. We will see that the brokenness of repentance is at the core of peacemaking as we contrast the two brothers. The life of the older brother stands in stark contrast with that of both the prodigal and the father.

65

As we look at the "religious spirit" of the older brother we will learn how religious self-righteousness can be an obstacle to peacemaking. The brokenness of the prodigal, which is contrasted with the pride of the older brother, is the first half of Jesus' story of peacemaking through repentance. We will see in the father a radical grace that is as extravagant in its display of joy and love as is the prodigal's extravagance in rebellion. It is this display of grace that is the other half of peacemaking.

Jesus offers the parable of the prodigal son to an audience that is probably more like the unforgiving older brother than the repentant prodigal or the loving father. The parable is about the father's grace, which stands in contrast to the older brother's pride and anger. The rebellious prodigal provides the context for the storyline, which is designed to challenge the popular but misguided older brothers in the audience. It also serves to assure the sinner of God's grace in the face of radical repentance that is modeled by the prodigal. The story also shows us how we can be peacemakers as it contrasts two brothers, one who is reconciled to his family and the other who is self-isolated from it. The story is told in Luke 15.

Luke 15:11–32

"11 Jesus continued: "There was a man who had two sons. 12 The younger one said to his father, 'Father, give me my share of the estate.' So he divided his property between them. 13 "Not long after that, the younger son got together all he had, set off for a distant country and there squandered his wealth in wild living. 14 After he had spent everything, there was a severe famine in that whole country, and he began to be in need. 15 So he went and hired himself out to a citizen of that country, who sent him to his fields to feed pigs. 16 He longed to fill his stomach with the pods that the pigs were eating, but no one gave him anything. 17 "When he came to his senses, he said, 'How many of my father's

---

hired men have food to spare, and here I am starving to death! 18 I will set out and go back to my father and say to him: Father, I have sinned against heaven and against you. 19 I am no longer worthy to be called your son; make me like one of your hired men.' 20 So he got up and went to his father. "But while he was still a long way off, his father saw him and was filled with compassion for him; he ran to his son, threw his arms around him and kissed him. 21 "The son said to him, 'Father, I have sinned against heaven and against you. I am no longer worthy to be called your son.' 22 "But the father said to his servants, 'Quick! Bring the best robe and put it on him. Put a ring on his finger and sandals on his feet. 23 Bring the fattened calf and kill it. Let's have a feast and celebrate. 24 For this son of mine was dead and is alive again; he was lost and is found.' So they began to celebrate. 25 "Meanwhile, the older son was in the field. When he came near the house, he heard music and dancing. 26 So he called one of the servants and asked him what was going on. 27 'Your brother has come,' he replied, 'and your father has killed the fattened calf because he has him back safe and sound.' 28 "The older brother became angry and refused to go in. So his father went out and pleaded with him. 29 But he answered his father, 'Look! All these years I've been slaving for you and never disobeyed your orders. Yet you never gave me even a young goat so I could celebrate with my friends. 30 But when this son of yours who has squandered your property with prostitutes comes home, you kill the fattened calf for him!' 31 "'My son,' the father said, 'you are always with me, and everything I have is yours. 32 But we had to celebrate and be glad, because this brother of yours was dead and is alive again; he was lost and is found.'"

This story is one of the most popular and memorable parables of Jesus. Most people in our culture know its general storyline but few have appreciated its deep implications with respect to repentance and grace. While the prodigal son is probably not the primary character of the story, he provides a powerful picture of the dynamics of genuine repentance. His story is our story in so many ways, as we will see.

In preparation for the upcoming chapters let's summarize and contrast the two brothers in this parable. Each has a story to tell that is timeless and applicable to people of all cultures. One of the reasons the parable has enjoyed such popularity is its universal relevance.

The Prodigal	*The Older Brother*
Outwardly rebellious	Outwardly obedient
Understood his neediness	Never saw his neediness
His brokenness led to wholeness	His pride kept him immature
In the end enjoyed the fellowship of the Father	In the end excluded himself from fellowship
The portrait of a spirit of repentance	The portrait of a religious spirit

If we are to find the peace that accompanies grace, and if we are to be peacemakers, we will need to learn lessons from the prodigal, the older brother, and the father. The prodigal's brokenness, the older brother's religious pride, and the father's graciousness each offer critical lessons to peacemakers. The way we choose to see ourselves and tell our story is critical to peace seeking and peacemaking. Too often we, like the Prodigal, tell a story of shame and worthlessness, or like the older brother, we see ourselves as entitled. We need to see ourselves through the eyes of the Father as recipients of grace who are then free to express that grace.

Peacemakers understand that repentance has more to do with returning home than it does with changing the way we conduct ourselves in "a distant land." We will not be reconciled to others while we are living in "a distant land" away from our spiritual home. The social peace that accompanies reconciliation takes place under the father's roof and as a part of the father's gracious reception. The father has much to show us about what it takes to be reconciled to those who have hurt us through foolish, selfish, sinful, behavior. The older brother will show us one of the great obstacles to peacemaking—religiosity. But it is the prodigal son who will show us the steps to true repentance.

Take the following inventory of your soul. Choose between the two statements "a" or "b." Which best describes your understanding?

1.
(a) I tend to keep score of my virtues and sacrifices expecting God to reward me.
(b) I simply do not think about what I have done for Christ and His kingdom.

2.
(a) I ask God for favors expecting that He will answer my prayers because I have been faithful to Him.
(b) I petition God expecting Him to care for me because of Christ apart from my faithfulness.

3.
(a) I do not feel I should associate with so-called believers who have serious sin in their lives.
(b) I am compassionate with other believers who have failed in their Christian walk because I know I have also failed or may fail.

4.
(a) I see all acts of selfishness as terrible sins that convict me of my need for grace.
(b) I don't think things like anger, jealousy, materialism, and envy are really bad sins.

5.
(a) I actually believe I have lived a pretty good life and deserve to be blessed.

(b) My blessings are not deserved and my sins are ever before me but I know I am forgiven and free.

6.

(a) I am angry or at least confused with God because He has not honored my sacrifices for Him.

(b) I love and praise God in spite of what happens.

7.

(a) I am willing to be honest with my failures even if it tarnishes my public image.

(b) My image is very important and I will work very hard to preserve it.

8.

(a) I believe Christians who have serious moral failures in life should be made to pay the price.

(b) I am eager to encourage sinners who own up to their failures and try hard to make things right.

9.

(a) Blessing and restoring serious sinners is generally not a good move in that it may encourage others to live undisciplined lives.

(b) It is really important to fully restore sinners lest they be left in shame and preyed upon by Satan.

10.

(a) Repentance is a deep process that is ongoing.

(b) Repentance is simply a matter of confessing sins.

NOTE:

The (a) statements represent a religious spirit while the (b) statements represent a penitent spirit in all but #4,7,10, where it is just the reverse.

Chapter 5
Pain, the Trailhead to Peace
Feeling the Heat Is Key to Seeing the Light

Step #4 to Peace with God:
Repentance

To experience peace with God and one another we
must experience true repentance, which starts with pain.

A young man shared with me his sad story of growing up in a home without a father. It was at a summer camp during his teen years that a Christian counselor befriended him and became something of a surrogate father to him. The relationship brought healing to deep wounds in this young man's life. But there came a time in the relationship where, through a tragic misunderstanding, this counselor turned away from his young friend and in doing so reopened the wounds that had been healing. The results were devastatingly painful but wonderfully redemptive. It was in this intense pain that the young man said, "It was then I realized only God could really be the father I longed for." When our strategies for finding life apart from God fail, we then have opportunity for deep repentance. Today this young man is in a ministry reaching others who are alone and vulnerable to the tragic mistake of looking for life in the wrong places. His is a story of repentance. It is not his misplaced hope or the rejection of his friend that would define him. It was his response to these things that would determine his ultimate fate. We will all sin. We will not all repent. It is not sin but repentance that determines our destiny. It is not only the selfish, wrong things that we do, but more so the noble, good things that we fail to do that constitute our problem.

Radical grace, the grace granted to God's redeemed, is based upon a radical sacrifice—the cross. Radical grace is also based on radical repentance and faith. What kind of repentance leads to salvation? Is true repentance focused primarily on forsaking our evil deeds, or is it concerned more with our failure to fill our lives with the right things?

Verses 11–21 of Luke 15 give us a portrait of the prodigal son and an insightful description of repentance. Faith that saves the soul is linked to repentance and is inauthentic without it. But the repentance that is a part of saving faith has often been misunderstood as focused on turning from disobedience to the moral demands of the law when it should more appropriately focus on changing our attitude toward Christ. This is not to suggest that "coming home" to Christ does not involve a radical change in motives, attitudes, and conduct. We will see that the prodigal left the distant land and corresponding lifestyle, but we will also see that the point of the parable is not his changed conduct so much as his changed address, attitude toward his father, and his true identity. It is not so much, what he gave up but rather what he embraced in its place that defined his repentance. Repentance is not so much the discipline to stop selfish, sinful behavior, as it is the displacement of sinful behavior with a wise, virtuous life.

What Constitutes the Core Problem of Life?

The profile of repentance starts with the prodigal taking control of his inheritance and *"journeying in a distant country"* (vs. 11–13). At the core of the prodigal's folly are not only his hedonistic lifestyle but also his desire to live on his own. Again the prophet Jeremiah reminds us, *"For My people have committed two evils: They have forsaken Me, the fountain of living waters, to hew for themselves cisterns, broken cisterns, that can hold no water"* (Jer. 2:13). At the core of our sin problem is the impulse to live our lives our way—to find happiness, wholeness, or even holiness through our own plans and power. Sin is the active search for the life of the kingdom apart from a relationship with the King. Repentance therefore involves not only addressing the foolish behavior of "hewing for ourselves broken cisterns" but also the "forsaking of God" as the source of life.

The prodigal was breaking the commandments by wasting his resources on harlotry and loose living. These were but tactical errors in his search for life, much in the same way that Eve ate of the forbidden fruit in the Garden of Eden believing it would be a better path to wholeness than obedience to God's Word. We, like the prodigal and Eve, are motivated (in our rebellion) not by a hatred of God and His Word so much as by a lack of confidence in both as a means of satisfying the deepest longings of our lives. At the root of our rebellion is a distrust of God and a misguided confidence in our own ability to manage life in order to find peace. This self-sufficient posture is the way of Satan.

The sin that typically gets attention is the story of the prodigal's breaking of the sixth commandment. The prodigal was foolishly wasting his inheritance on immoral living. But there is another dimension to the prodigal's sin. It is his strategic dislocation. He was looking for life in a distant land. He was breaking the first commandment. The sin that really besets us is the temptation to believe that God is not enough. Was not this at the root of Eve's problem as well?

Our distant land might very well be our vocation, family, ministry, parents, or our health. When something other than Jesus takes on a messianic role in our lives, we are in danger of following the path of the prodigal son. Anything in this world that we believe will give us "life" or ease the pain of our soul's sorrow may constitute an idol, a false Messiah. Our functional Messiah is anything that makes us feel alive. Too often Jesus is only a figurehead Messiah while something else is our functional Messiah.

When our youngest son was four years old, his six-year-old sister talked to him about the gospel. After explaining the story of Jesus in her own way, she asked him this question, "David, when you die do you want to go to heaven to be with Jesus, God, Mommy, Daddy, and big sister, or do you want to go to the lake of fire to be with the devil and robbers?" After a contemplative pause David said, "I want to stay right here." After a long laugh, I thought about my son's answer and realized he could be speaking for a whole lot of us. We have no lack of hunger for the blessings of the kingdom of God in this life—peace, justice, prosperity, and joy. It is the King we seem to have a problem with. We balk at His call to bear a cross in this life and await His crown in the next. We don't want to die and go to heaven or hell. We want heaven to come here ASAP.

> ### *A point to ponder*
>
> Our functional Messiah can be anything that makes us feel alive.

We have our own strategies to bring in the kingdom. To the extent these strategies are not centered on God's plan, they call for repentance. James asks, *"What is the source of quarrels and conflicts among you?"* Our strategic sins like independence, self-centeredness, and pride lead us to tactical sins like immorality, social conflict, and bitterness. True repentance must address more than tactical outward behavior. Repentance that does not bring the prodigal home is a superficial repentance. It is of little value for the prodigal to start over in the distant land with a more sophisticated strategy of independent living. He is not better off by taking his inheritance and investing it in good stocks or even social service. He is still dislocated and living independent of his father.

The prodigal's story starts with trying to find life in a distant land on his own apart from his father. I can't overstate this point. We too often try to change the way we invest our resources in a distant land and call it repentance. We need to change our address—go home and renew our confidence in Christ as Messiah, Lord, and King. When I "repent" of losing my temper and yet fail to address my selfish expectations that set up my anger, I have not really repented. I more likely have repressed the anger only to have it come out in some other way, an ulcer perhaps. The typical marquee sins of popular culture—immorality, covetousness, and self-worship are but tactical investments of resources in a distant land. The root of the sin is independence from God, an insistence on being in control, of doing it my way, and of defining the meaning of "abundant life" by the world's values. We may change our moral conduct and not move one inch toward true repentance, toward our spiritual home.

A point to ponder

The greatest challenge to the emotionally
ill is not unrealistic behavior
but unrealistic perceptions.
The same is true of the spiritually ill.

The first move the prodigal son makes is away from his father and his true home. This independent rebellion sets the context for true repentance. Rebellion can be overt and dramatic as in the case of the prodigal, or it can be more subtle and sophisticated as in the case of the older brother who lives at home but is seeking his life through his own efforts. In both cases we must look behind the superficial expressions of our spiritual rebellion to the core spirit of independence from God our Father.

The Setting
Vs.11–13 **Independent Rebellion**
Deep longings for life + sinful strategies =
"Journeying in a distant country"

The first step in the prodigal's repentance and ours is seen in verses 14–16 of Luke 15. Here he experiences intense pain. He senses his "need" and experiences deep "longing." Does God want us to succeed? Not in a distant land, he doesn't. God may welcome our humiliation and failure if it will bring us to our senses. God is not as interested in preserving our reputation as we would like Him to be. Nor is He interested in removing all discomfort and pain from our lives. What we label as the attack of the enemy on our right to abundant life may be the hand of God shattering our idols. The loss and pain in the prodigal's life were a blessing in disguise. How often are we praying that God would grant us success in the distant land meanwhile wondering why God has not helped us acquire the "desire of our carnal heart?"

My work with inmates from a local prison has put me in contact with some dramatic stories of repentance and redemption. One inmate who was a male nurse had a patient die under his care. He was convicted of first-degree murder based on a supposed "confession" and is serving a life sentence. As I looked at the court record of his trial, it appeared to me that he had been wrongly convicted; but I have never heard this person complain about his story. He told me that if he had had O.J. Simpson's dream team defending him, God would have still seen that he got a conviction because God knew it would take that to get his attention.

A point to ponder

It is not our sins and circumstances that define our character so much as our response to them.

Secondary Pain

God often allows pain to show us that we need to come home. But sometimes the pain can be avoided or medicated so we don't get the message. It is in these circumstances that a loving God orders up what I call "secondary pain." This is discipline that is inflicted by loved ones, so I will not continue to pursue foolish strategies in my search for life. In 1 Corinthians 5:1–5 Paul talks about church discipline being used as an instrument of redemptive pain when the natural consequences of sin are not quickly forthcoming.

When our kids were younger, we told them; "When you ride a bike, you wear a helmet; when you walk, you don't need one. If you are riding a bike without a helmet, you are indicating you would rather walk." Grounding kids for not wearing a helmet is not an act of cruelty or harassment but of love. In some cases the natural consequences are so severe we don't want to allow them to take place in order to learn the lesson. In such cases we create artificial circumstances that are not as traumatic but painful enough to teach. There is an important principle here. The proper place for church discipline or family discipline is when there is an unrepentant contentment with living in a distant land that is independent of God. As we will see in the story of the prodigal son, repentance is linked to feeling the consequences of our foolish strategies for finding life.

"Grow Antennae, not Horns."

Several years ago while in the Caribbean I expected to get some great shopping bargains. I went into a store that advertised Leica binoculars at a 40 percent discount. What a deal! I recognized Leica as quality but did not know many details about the particular product I was buying. I felt I had made a great decision. When I returned home and looked on the Internet, I found the same product for many dollars less. I learned a lesson—not all sales are good deals. Now to be sure the pain involved was not great, but it was great enough that I never forgot it. My rather trivial shopping experience conditioned my behavior so that such a mistake would probably not happen again. Pain, even slight discomfort, can be a powerful teacher. While this incident was rather trivial, there would be many more severe experiences of pain in my life and ministry that would provide powerful opportunities for learning. We must always remember that our failures or the missteps of others are not so critical as our response to those sins. Our response to sin and failure starts with experiencing pain. Spiritual sociopaths don't repent because they don't feel the pain of their foolish decisions. Dr. James R. Angell, the first president of Yale University was asked, "What is the key to success?" His response was simple, "Grow antennae, not horns." I have found that when I am in touch with my spiritual need for grace I am not a "picky eater" spiritually. A spiritually healthy person is easily edified even when the sermons, worship music, social company, life circumstances, etc. are not exactly what they might prefer. They see life as a series of opportunities not as a series of obstacles.

A point to ponder

A healthy Christian is easily edified.

"What Goes Around Comes Around."

When Jesus said, "*Judge not lest you be judged*," he was saying, "What goes around, comes around." The way we treat others is the way others will treat us. Now if we are smart or "have ears to hear," we "get it." In the case of the story of the graceless servant (look ahead to ch.9), there was a painful lesson to be learned. He did not treat others lovingly as he was treated, so now he would be treated similarly to become empathetic. Was this cruel and unusual punishment, or was it a necessary and loving act of discipline? It could be either depending on the motives of the teacher. In Hebrews 12 we read that God disciplines those

He loves. For that reason we should not fight but rather welcome correction and teaching that will enable us to develop empathy so we can participate in God's community, not missing out on the benefits of His Kingdom.

I recall an experience early in my pastoral work where a young mother talked to me about how difficult it was for her family to be involved in our church because they lived forty minutes away and were living on a very restricted budget. I inquired as to why she had not considered a relationship with one of the many good churches nearer her home. Later I discovered that in response to our conversation she was devastated and cried for two days. I thought I was being helpful by not being possessive of her involvement in our church. Several years after this experience I finally "got it." I found myself outside my own church family sensing that the leadership in the church was not interested in whether I stayed or left. It was painful to feel unwanted, insignificant, and unappreciated. Interestingly my thoughts went back to my conversation with this young mother. I could now, after all this time, understand and empathize with her. How many other dear people had I hurt by the unintended message that they were really not wanted, important, or valued by the church family and me? The lesson of this painful experience of "discipline" was burned into my life so that from that time on I always assumed one of the most important messages anyone in a church wants and needs to hear is the message, "We want you, need you, value you, and care about you." Empathy is the part of love that builds community. Discipline is the part of love that teaches empathy. Courageous faith is the part of love that exercises discipline. And all of this builds a peacemaker.

In *Peace Seekers* I spoke of a young inmate with whom I had a relationship. He had come to a renewal of his faith while serving an eleven-year sentence for drug addiction and forgery. He had lost his marriage, kids, career, and reputation. But he had gained and displayed a peace that seemed supernatural given his circumstances. I never detected a note of bitterness or resentment for what I thought to be a very stiff sentence for his crimes. What he did share with me was the grace of God that had become more than a doctrine. It had become a living fire in his life. He told me, "I will leave this prison with more than I brought in. My losses were great but my gains are greater."

This inmate not only had a new awareness of God's grace toward himself but also a new empathy and compassion for fellow prisoners he had previously ignored or despised. He was grateful for the chance imprisonment gave him to rid himself of an addiction to painkilling drugs. He had a new vision for an after-school ministry that would help kids stay off the streets, noting that was where so many of his fellow prisoners lost their way. While longing to be reconciled with his family, he realized his peace could not be tied to the realization of those hopes. It was the grace of God that brought him peace with God and empathy for others. He is now a peacemaker.

Some of us do not respond to the discipline of pain and learn. In our situations it may take repeated experiences of pain to wake us up. Those who never seem to get it may stay in the unfortunate state of restlessness, anxiety, self-absorption, and depression. It is at such a position of being stuck that church discipline plays a role. In the third appendix of this book we explore the dynamics of church discipline, which is too often ignored or poorly practiced.

We cannot change what we do not acknowledge as needing change. A vital step to true repentance is pain, which can be God's way of telling us that something needs attention. To be sure there are many causes of pain in our lives and not all of them are because of our sin. It is a good bet however to see in our pain (from whatever the cause) a challenge to make spiritual adjustments. Pain will bring a response drawing us to God or leading us away from Him.

Edification is the objective of the church community, but it cannot take place until the individual is willing to be edified. Those who have ears to hear will hear. Those who are hungry will be nourished. Those who are motivated to come home will find the path and follow it. The next chapter will offer further insight into this process of real change.

The Depth of our Pain is related to the Height of our Experience of Grace.

If we spend our lives resisting the discipline, killing the pain, and "cooking the books" of our story, we will inevitably stunt our spiritual growth. Repentance seldom takes place at a deep level without feeling the pain of sin at a deep level. Where sin abounds, grace does all the more abound. Where pain abounds, true repentance all the more can abound. If the pain is shallow, we will tend never to leave the distant land but just reload and try to make life work at this foreign address while on our own.

Step #1
vs. 14–16 pain
"need", "longing"

Those who experience the grace of God at a level that motivates obedience are inevitably the same people who have felt the pain of life without God. This presents an interesting scenario. To have lived a "relatively" pain free life may also mean that one misses some of the deep riches and power of God's grace. The Gospel is good news for sinners—those who have made bad decisions and suffered as a result. It is not that we should seek to be spiritual rebels like the prodigal son in order to experience radical grace. It does mean that like the prodigal son we see the depth of our neediness and not lose sight of the power of superficial holiness to keep us from intimacy with God. Moral discipline is a virtue until it becomes prideful independence from God.

81

Steps to Application

1. Take an inventory of your struggle with sin in a particular area of life. Try to identify the core sin and how it is expressed outwardly in your life.

2. Most of us are in some kind of relationship where we may be responsible for exercising some form of discipline on others. Think through how you might constructively handle it.

3. Reflect on how you have responded to hardships in your life. Note things you now see as counter productive in your response and some specific corrections that will encourage you to not repeat the mistakes in your response.

4. Ask yourself how you have responded to pain in your life. How would you evaluate the wisdom of your response? How can your response be improved?

Questions for Discussion

1. What is the hardest part of administering discipline? Why?

2. What is the hardest part of receiving discipline? Why?

3. How have you seen church discipline mishandled or handled well?

4. What has been the spiritual effect of pain in your life?

5. How has pain affected your life, and how have you grown through it or had growth stifled by it?

6. Are there parts of this chapter with which you disagree? Why?

Chapter 6
No Peace away from Home
Seeing the Light and Following it Home

Repentance starts with Insight and ends with Action

Let me ask you a question. If a student strives to please her father by getting good grades, and she cheats on an exam to get an "A"; what will it look like for her to "come to her senses" and repent? Some might say, "She needs to confess her cheating as sin and commit herself not to do it again." I would suggest that "coming to her senses" also involves seeing that her drive to please her father might be a "distant land" that needs to be challenged. But someone will quickly remind me that children should desire to please their parents. This certainly cannot be regarded as sinful can it? If she is seeking to find personal significance and security for her soul through her father's love to the extent she would cheat to get it, there is a deeper problem than cheating going on. We have in this case another example of idolatry. To repeat Jeremiah's words, *"For My people have committed two evils: They have forsaken Me, the fountain of living waters, to hew for themselves cisterns, broken cisterns, that can hold no water."* Repentance for this young girl will involve 1.) dealing with the cheating, and 2.) dealing with the sin of looking to her father for what only God can provide—a deep sense of self-worth that goes beyond good grades or worldly approval. We are looking at a young girl whose real problem is her living in a distant land away from the security of her heavenly father's love.

Pain can push us in one of four directions. First, we can develop strategies to remove or medicate the pain with painkillers including addictive substances and obsessive behaviors. These strategies too often lead to more trouble because they treat only the symptoms. Second, we can become hopeless—seeing no way out of our condition.

Third, we can become bitter—taking the posture of a victim while we blame others. Fourth, we can gain insight and see the light.

What does it take for someone to "get it?" Without the proper insight genuine repentance will not happen. In the last chapter we spoke of pain as an important part of the repentance process. But pain will only be beneficial if it leads to the second step toward true repentance—insight. It might be helpful to refresh your memory of the story of the prodigal son by going back and rereading Luke 15.

Insight

This second step in the prodigal's repentance and ours is seen in Luke 15 verse 17. The prodigal *"came to his senses."* The Greek word for "repentance" is a compound of two other words that mean, "to perceive afterwards." The meaning of the word is illustrated in the prodigal's story. Repentance involves a perception change.

Step #2
vs. 17 **insight**
"come to his senses"

Several years ago while traveling in Asia I spent some time on a ferry traveling from Hong Kong to Macau. My spirit was as gray as the weather that day. I felt alone and discouraged as I reflected on some painful events in my life. My pity party progressed and I prayed asking God, "Why couldn't things have been different?" And as I sat there not expecting an answer, I was suddenly struck by these words that slipped into my mind (I assume by the Holy Spirit). They were something like this, "Let me show you how things might have been had I not intervened. I will assure you it is not going to be pretty. I called all who would follow Me to serve selflessly and even to suffer. So why are you sad when I ask you to do what I have done and what you agreed (at your baptism) you would do?" I had to confess I was not taking my baptism into Christ seriously, but God was. I recognized that I died to myself in the water of baptism but had not expected to enter a life that would actually involve real sacrifice. I was expecting a marriage, family, career, etc. that was "abundant" without so much self-sacrifice.

These thoughts were powerful and healing. Within minutes I had a very different perspective and attitude. It was as though I had been reminded of something I had forgotten, an insight that offered healing. Repentance was taking place. My outward posture of disbelief, frustration, anger, and resentment evaporated not because I attacked these feelings as evil but rather because I came to see things differently. I experienced a renewal of my mind, a change in my perception as a result of coming to my senses. This is a normal, essential, part of true repentance.

A point to ponder

Failure is not an event
so much as an opinion.

The insight step is another area where we often need the help of the Christian community. We need to be taught the true meaning of spiritual warfare and how the enemy can let us repent of the superficial sins while we continue to practice and even encourage the underlying sins. We need people with insight who are able to speak the truth in love to us. People we trust will continue to accept and love us even when they don't approve of what we are doing. People like the prophet Nathan who can say, *"Thou art the man"* (2 Sam.12:1–7) as he confronts King David over his sins of adultery and murder. It is interesting to note how often Jesus' teaching seems to be aimed at bringing insight. For example, how often did He conclude a teaching with, *"He who has an ear to hear, let him hear"?* To be wiser we must not only have light but also sight. Too many of us are bathed in light but have no sight. We need to pray that our eyes be opened to see (Eph.1:18).

Sociologist Christian Smith described American spirituality as "moralistic, therapeutic deism." The new tendency among Americans (including many Christians) is to see the human problem as dysfunction more than sin. Jesus is pictured not so much as a savior from the curse of the law but as a life coach who leads us to a better marriage, happier kids, and greater success in the race for the American dream. Or to put it in the framework of the prodigal's story, many of us expect the father to come to our aid in the distant land and help us better manage our inheritance. Satan does not mind people being blessed so long as they never realize they are still heavily invested in the world. As long as we can be kept from the pain that leads to insight, we remain unrepentant. We may think that Satan wants us to be in pain while he may rather want us to live our lives in a superficial happiness apart from God.

Commitment

> ### *Step #3*
> vs. 18–19 **commitment**
> *"I will", "I am"*

The third step in repentance is commitment to a different goal. This step is illustrated in verses 18–19. The prodigal is not just trying harder to manage his life "in a distant land." The prodigal said, "I will go home." He sees that his real need is to "leave this land and get home." How often does the call to commitment in our Christian churches sound like "try harder" as opposed to "change your spiritual address"? Change must take place on two levels—first, the strategic or big picture level, and second, the tactical or more superficial level. The prodigal made a strategic change when he decided to get up and go home. He could have made only a tactical change by saying, "Send more money," or "The devil is trying to rob me or ruin my day by keeping me from reaching my goals over here in a far land." It is possible for the prodigal to turn from his foolish hedonistic exploits only to reinvest in the stock market or even in social ministry but still be lost in a distant land.

Certainly wise investing in the stock market (or ministry) is better than foolish investing in selfish, worldly living; but is repentance on this level really getting at the core issue? Or are we looking at simply a different strategy to find life apart from home? When someone is drunk on wine, we may kick him out of our congregation; but if he is drunk on money, we may make him a deacon. Drunkenness is a sin whether it is on wine that robs us of our senses or on money that represents an idolatrous hope. Much of what we call repentance in our churches is little more than suffering the consequences of our superficial foolishness, realizing we need to change something without altering the basic understanding of where we will find life. We are still refusing to leave the distant land, trying to find life in our work while serving two masters. We cling to whatever it is that gives us earthly comfort or makes us feel alive at the moment. It seems to me God takes a great risk every time He blesses us. The risk is that we will run off to worship the blessing and forget that He alone is the source of life.

Action

> ### *Step #4*
> vs. 20–21 **action**
> *"he left the distant land"*

Step four in the repentance chain is found in verses 20–21 of Luke 15: "*He got up (left the distant land) and came to his father.*" The action step puts the insight to practical use. The prodigal son went home, confessed his sin, humbled himself, and received the father's gracious love. Open confession of our sin, swallowing our pride, and humbling ourselves are the appropriate fruits of repentance. We must stop supporting and making excuses for the foolish "cisterns" we have created that cannot hold water. The grace of the father was not experienced until action was taken—coming home. Grace did not come at the point of pain, insight, or the commitment to act. The father withheld his blessing until he saw action.

A point to ponder

The mind sets our direction and the heart gives us the energy to move.

Leaving the distant land was the action step that counted. The father does not mention the specific sins of the prodigal in the distant land. His address was the issue. "Getting up" (vs.20) suggests the prodigal may have been discouraged and even passively depressed in his fallen condition. He needed to get it together enough to take the action step. He was not going to be rescued. *He* was the one who went to the "far land." Now *he* would have to be the one who would pick himself up and find his way home.

What might the action step look like for us today? Open expressions of humility will almost always be involved. If we are not willing to be humbled in the face of our foolish strategies, we probably have not really repented. Saving face is not a part of the negotiations in true repentance. My experience suggests it is too easy to try to avoid or at least modify this step with some kind of defensive explanation for our behavior. The prodigal offers no explanation. There is no recounting of early childhood trauma. There is no playing "the victim card." There is no story of being caught in a "weak moment." The action step is bold, defenseless, and simple. When we try to offer an explanation for our behavior, it too often comes off sounding like an excuse. We are better off making a clean break with our old address and moving on. Everyone who has strayed and repents has a story to tell, but the fourth step is not the place for telling the story. That will come much later, if at all.

The Dynamics of Repentance from Luke 15:11-21

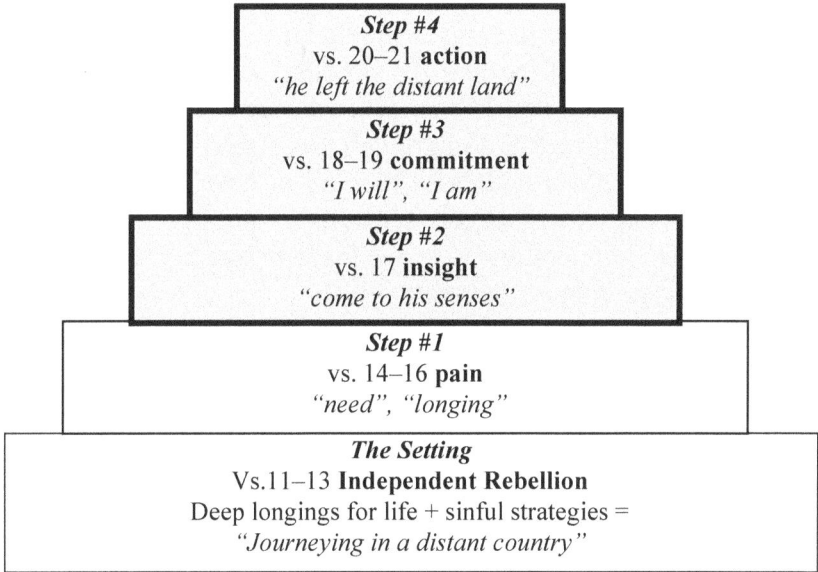

| **Step #4** |
| vs. 20–21 **action** |
| *"he left the distant land"* |

| **Step #3** |
| vs. 18–19 **commitment** |
| *"I will", "I am"* |

| **Step #2** |
| vs. 17 **insight** |
| *"come to his senses"* |

| **Step #1** |
| vs. 14–16 **pain** |
| *"need", "longing"* |

| **The Setting** |
| Vs.11–13 **Independent Rebellion** |
| Deep longings for life + sinful strategies = |
| *"Journeying in a distant country"* |

Grace is not Inconsistent with Repentance

The spirit of grace is not to be confused with a punitive spirit of legalistic religion, which forgets about the cross. The punitive spirit always seeks to bring pain to the life of a sinner even after the sinner has repented. Creating guilt feelings—not to be confused with conviction—is not a part of the father's agenda in this parable. The father has no penalty box or booth in purgatory for the repentant son. Nor is grace to be confused with the permissive spirit of relativism, which forgets about repentance. The story of the prodigal calls for the display of radical grace only after the son has come to radical repentance. The father does not go to the distant land to rescue the prodigal. We might say the spirit of grace is the purifying spirit of redemption, which remembers the cross and calls us to come home. The peace of God comes to those who experience true repentance. If we are to be peacemakers, we will have to preach and practice true repentance and genuine forgiveness.

Incomplete Repentance

There are many examples of incomplete repentance. "I'm sorry I hurt your feelings. I should have said it in a different way." This may be like the prodigal saying, "I'm sorry I wasted the money. If you give me some more, I will be wiser next time." We might call this superficial repentance because it never addresses the distant land issue. It is like the person who repents of cheating to get a good grade but doesn't quit looking to a personal image as a means of finding security and success in life.

Then there is the example of what we might call conditional repentance. It sees the need to go home but not with humility. "You better kill the fatted calf now that I am back because if you don't, that means you don't really love me." This is like the husband who wants back into his abusive relationship with his wife for the eighth time just because he said he was sorry. The prodigal's spirit was not a spirit of entitlement. It was unconditional surrender to the righteous judgment of the Father. There was no spirit of negotiating a noble salvation of the soul's ego with a demand that there be mercy, love, or respect offered to the prodigal. The prodigal was through with himself.

Another example of incomplete repentance is what we might call intellectual repentance. It makes mental gestures in the direction of true insight but never gets around to doing anything about a change in behavior. You know the well-worn line, "You can talk the talk but can you walk the walk?" Sometimes people equate the confession of sin with repentance. This is certainly a grave mistake if by confession we mean little more than intellectual acknowledgment of a wrong done.

Self-centered repentance is another common error. It tries to make things right by human effort without a deep brokenness before God. It says, "I made a mess of things, and I will make it up to you." The implication is that if I can make atonement for my sins, I will then be free from any shame or guilt. While there is plenty of room for restitution in much of our sinning, restitution is no substitute for brokenness before God. It is not enough to just balance the books of wrongs with rights. I must acknowledge and deal with the brokenness of my own soul before God. My sins can be opportunities to see myself in a way that will move me toward my spiritual home. Repentance is what brings me there.

A point to ponder

It is hard to learn without listening.
It is hard to listen while talking.

The Renewed Mind

True repentance involves a renewing of the mind, a returning to our home, and a reception of the consequences. These consequences involve our posture of humility and our intimacy with a gracious God. Because grace is motivated by love, not tolerance or permissiveness, it has one agenda: edification. Love expressed through grace usually brings one of two responses. It melts a person's heart and leads to healing, or it drives a person to further foolishness and sin. This means that grace involves a great risk. There will be those who take advantage of it and abuse it. In doing so they harden their hearts. Justice that is centered in the cross, not in our performance or experience, also motivates attraction to God's grace. We cannot make up for our sins, nor will we always be treated fairly. We can only acknowledge our sins, receive God's forgiveness, and live lives in worshipful gratitude.

All of us are in need of repeated repentance. We need to ask ourselves if we are in touch with the pain that can lead to insight? Not all pain is the result of rebellion or foolish wandering in spiritual distant lands, but much more of it can be related to our sin than we want to admit. Don't be afraid of emotional pain. It can be a window for blessing. The open gashes in our heart are entry points for God's Spirit. Maybe we know the pain but not the insight it could produce. When this is the case, we need to pray for insight and for an ear to hear. We need to make it safe for our Christian friends to share with us and even confront us when needed with the insight they may have for us. If we are blessed with insight into what must change in our lives, we then need to "just do it." Make a commitment to take a step toward home.

A point to ponder

True repentance is a call to come home,
not just to manage our inheritance
more wisely.

When we think of Job's friend, we think of "friends" who wrongly assume that pain in a life is the result of sin in that life. This is of course a very superficial analysis of life, but it too often happens. I mention this for a rather strange reason. Don't dismiss "Job's friends" in your life too quickly. They may be an irritation, but then again they may have a point. As a wise person once told me, "Everyone's criticism deserves at least *some* serious consideration." Even when we sense their motives are not right, God may want to use them to tell us something we cannot see ourselves. I have found if I am serious about growing in my faith, I must expect the discipline of repentance to be a part of my Christian walk. My response to life's circumstances and the critique of others is the key to any spiritual progress.

Repentance that Justifies and Sanctifies

There are two spheres of repentance in the Christian experience. The repentance that leads to justification is repentance from the sin of "dead works." It is a transfer of hope from self to Christ. It is conversion from my soul's faith in anything and everything but Christ to trust in Christ alone. Repentance in this sphere is not so much a turning away from specific sins like immorality, covetousness, or substance abuse. It is repentance from one strategic sin—the pride of self-righteousness, which says I do not trust Christ as my righteousness.

Within the Christian life there is a daily need for a second kind of repentance from specific sins of disobedience to the will and law of God. This second sphere of repentance has nothing to do with our justification. It is a part of our ongoing sanctification process. We will need to repeatedly exercise this second kind of repentance as we stumble through life and wander away from our true spiritual home. The repentance that leads to life through union with Christ however is made once and for all. It need not be repeated every time we miss the mark (Heb.6:1-8).

The Two Spheres of Repentance

Justification	*Sanctification*
Repentance from dead works (pride of self righteousness) to faith in Christ's righteousness	Repentance from sinful habits to a walk that conforms to the glory of God
Turning from self (generally) to Christ	Turning from specific sins to obedience
Mk. 1:15; Heb. 6:1	2 Cor. 12:21

Outer and Inner Repentance

True repentance has an inward and outward aspect. First, we are convinced in our minds that we are lost away from home and need to change our spiritual address. This step may not be as simple as it seems because we are often unaware of the root of our rebellious independence. From early childhood we learn self-defensive strategies to justify our sinful and destructive responses to life. These defenses can be so deeply imbedded and hidden in our souls that we need help in exposing them. Pain has a way of forcing us to dig deep into our inner life so as to repent of our root sins. I sense that most of us give little attention to finding the root expression of our sins. Like much of modern medicine we medicate the symptoms. The addict finds ways to kick the habit without really understanding that the drug or alcohol was killing pain that was tied to trying to find peace in the wrong places and through the wrong channels.

Intellectual acknowledgement is one thing, but it must be accompanied by a deep conviction if step #2 will take place. The knowledge of sin cannot be superficial if it is to produce repentance. Our motivation must come from the heart. While the mind may determine the direction we go, it is the heart that gives us the energy to move. The inner posture of heart-felt conviction will push us to the more challenging steps.

The second step is the humiliation of admitting we have sinned and openly facing the shame of such a confession. Again the words of confession must come from a soul that is contrite. Words can be cheap even when they involve public humiliation. If we are not ready to leave the distant land, the confession will not lead to step #3. A contrite heart is a broken heart that is able to feel the weight of guilt, shame, loss, and damage caused by sin. People who have repressed their feelings from childhood so as to avoid such pain will face a special challenge. It may take some loving discipline from the community to bring to the surface the feelings of contrition that provide energy for real change.

Step three is the point of bearing the fruit of repentance. This step may involve making restitution to those who have been hurt. It may involve the loss of material position and possessions. It may include seeking help to overcome sinful and destructive perceptions and habits. This final change has an internal component, which is just as important as the external. This internal conversion has to do with our "motives," our "desires." If we are to find peace, we must have no unfinished business with respect to our spiritual address. We must truly repent and come home. The following chart summarizes the three steps described above.

	Step #1	*Step #2*	*Step #3*
Outer posture	**Convinced in mind** **Mk. 1:15**	**Confession of mouth** **Matt. 3:11**	**Conformity of walk** **Acts 26:20**
Inner posture	**Convicted in heart**	**Contrition of soul** **2 Cor. 7:10**	**Conversion of life** **Matt. 3:8**

Those who wish to be peacemakers need to understand that the three steps outlined above are an important part not only of one's inner personal peace but also in reconciliation of social relationships.

Steps to Application

1. Where does it hurt in your life? Ask yourself if the pain reveals any misplaced hopes and investments.

2. Be careful that you are not medicating pain to avoid more important issues. Ask yourself how you are responding to your pain.

3. Think through how you would like to respond should you ever be confronted or disciplined.

4. Check to see if your life is being lived in a distant land (away from your spiritual home). Use the following questions to guide you.

   a. Do you experience anxiety, anger, frustration, and bitterness that disrupt your peace?

    b. Do you find yourself making decisions that draw you away from what you know to be God's agenda for your life?

    c. Are you justifying your selfish behavior, believing God is making you "successful" in the world's eyes?

    d. Are you growing closer to a God centered life?

5. Maintain a regular devotional life centered on your relationship with Christ, not your success in life or your personal goals.

6. Expect and prepare for discipline and repentance if you are serious about growth.

Questions for Discussion

1. What is your distant land?

2. Can you give examples of true and false repentance in your own life?

3. How would you summarize this chapter?

4. Are there parts of this chapter with which you disagree? Why?

Chapter 7
No Chip Off the Old Block

Obstacle #4 to Peace with God: A Religious Spirit

*Peacemakers replace
the religious spirit with a gracious spirit.*

I will never forget the T-shirt I saw in a Boulder, Colorado shop that had the big letters "JESUS SAVE ME" on the front and just below in smaller print "from your followers." Ouch! Christian subculture can be toxic to the human soul. It can be hostile to our inner and outer life. It is sad, but many people who have been recipients of grace are not dispensers of grace. I'm talking about *true* Christians but not true Christianity. If we are to be peacemakers, we must be sure that our offensiveness comes from the Word of the Cross not from our lack of sensitivity.

To understand the older brother in the story of the prodigal son, we must see him in contrast to the father. This parable is really about the father who displays radical grace. The story addresses the older brothers in the audience who have what we might call "a religious spirit." By looking at the spirit of the Father we will see a contrast with the older brother. Both individuals will tell us a lot about making peace through grace.

Lessons from the Prodigal's Father (Luke 15:20–24)

The story of the Prodigal son takes a shocking turn at the point where the father enters the scene. Religion in Jesus' day could be harsh, and God was often seen as demanding more than forgiving. Things were hard for Israelites in Palestine when this parable was spoken. People were unfaithful, and the leaders tried to hold the fort by appealing to God's harsh judgment of sinners. Whenever the holy character of God is emphasized without a proper understanding of His love and mercy, a spirit of legalism emerges with guilt, fear, hypocrisy, and pride.

How might the prodigal's father have greeted his son? He might have said, "You have burned your bridges and hurt your mother and me to the point where there is no place for you here anymore." Or perhaps, "We are glad to see you come back, but you must understand you will have to earn your way into this family." Or maybe even, "We are overjoyed at your return, and we have a place for you; but I'm not sure we can ever trust you again." In this story the graciousness of the father is radical. His heart longs to see the son return. He spares nothing in celebrating his joy. He seems to forget all of the offenses. The word "prodigal" means wasteful extravagance. Just as the son wasted his inheritance, so the father was extravagant to the point of seeming wasteful with his graciousness. We have here the story of two prodigals, a son and a father.

Four Characteristics of the Father's Grace

Herein do we see four characteristics of the graciousness of the father. First, he was not overly possessive of his son or his property. He gave the son freedom to choose. He let the son go away and do it his way. Similarly God lets us go so we might grow. God has given us life and gifts, and we are free to use them in any way we choose. But this freedom is in reality a test.

When my wife and I first were faced with the harsh reality of our son's autism, we were stunned and thrown into confusion. It was as though the son we thought we had no longer lived. He died—or our image of him died. The son we really had was a person we could not imagine and may never know. Over a period of several years I was forced to give up my son to God's care and lay aside all my former expectations of him. This painful transaction proved to be a blessing in an unexpected way. As I mentioned earlier, this made it easier for me to give up an unhealthy possessiveness of my other two children as well.

As a parent I have learned I must give up a possessive attitude toward my kids if I am going to enable them to mature. This of course takes place over time as they grow. We did not let our children make many of their own decisions when they were three, but little by little we let them step out so by the time they were in their late teens they had considerable freedom. This was because they had developed a sense of responsibility as they gradually earned more and more freedom. They are now adults starting their own families, and it has been a wonderful experience to watch them travel the world and raise their own children. We took a risk in taking our hand off early, but in our case it was rewarded. When our youngest son and daughter left for college, they were ready to be on their own and capable of making sound decisions for themselves. To be sure they would make mistakes, but we knew that they would be wiser and stronger because they were allowed to act freely.

Sometimes we would like to have God hold on to us more tightly than He would chose to. An important part of our growth is related to Him letting us make our own decisions. Gracious people do not cling to or control others; they let go. I suspect the father in this parable could have easily prevented the son from making all those foolish choices simply by not permitting him to leave. But what would have been the result—maybe a carbon copy to the "older brother"? The fact that the father was not overly possessive set the stage for the younger son to grow up in a way the older brother did not.

The second thing we can say about this gracious father is that he was not overly protective. He did not prevent the son from making a mistake and suffering the consequences. This might seem neglectful to some of us. When a child is sexually abused, or when a drunk driver paralyzes a person, we ask, "Why did God allow this to happen? Where was God?" But if this tragedy causes a person to discover that our hope is in God not in what God does for us, do we still consider God abusive?

Gracious people understand the constructive role of pain and disappointment. They do not rush to rescue others from all suffering because they know that some of our spiritual growth comes from trials. As I often tell young couples preparing for marriage, "If you have a less than ideal marriage, you may become bitter, rebellious, and abusive; or you can find a deep relationship with God that you would not know if your marriage was perfect." After all the people closest to us are sometimes a spiritual distraction by playing a role in our lives that God alone deserves. More than one husband, wife, child, parent, pastor, and friend have functioned as a "Messiah surrogate," giving a sense of life to our souls. God takes a risk whenever He blesses us, for we can take the blessing and worship it rather than Him.

As parents sometimes we should let our children experience painful consequences early to learn a lesson. I remember my first experience buying a car. I had saved my money for several years and was dropped off at a dealership by my father who came back thirty minutes later to pick me up. The first thing I told the salesman was how much money I had to spend on a car. He knew he had a "cream puff"—a sucker who has no idea what is going on in a dealership. This is where car salesmen make their profit. Well let me tell you, I have learned a lot about buying cars over the last several years; and it all started that day when I was thrown to the wolves. I look back on that experience as a wise investment on my father's part. Better to be abused early and learn than to be in your forties and still not know how to deal for a car. But isn't it better to learn from wise advice rather than experience? Perhaps, but I must say, experience is a great teacher. I believe there are three kinds of parents. There are "bodyguards," "lifeguards," and "swimming instructors." The "bodyguards" never let the kids near the pool of life. The "lifeguards" are quick to pull them out when they fall in. But the "swimming instructors" are willing to get in the water and teach them to swim. The wise parent will want to teach a child to swim as early as possible, but this will mean resisting the temptation to isolate the child from all danger or rescue the child from all difficulties. Children will not learn to swim without getting wet.

The third characteristic of this gracious father was that he was not overly punitive. He did not penalize the son for failing. God is not as quick to punish, as we often fear. I meet many people who act as though God is just waiting for an excuse to slap them around. God does not punish penitent children. God does not treat you like a second-class member of His family because you have sinned. If you have not learned from your sin, He may discipline you so that you will be wiser but He does not exact punishment for that was already exhausted at the cross.

A woman in our congregation had grown up in a tragic home that included satanic rituals with sexual abuse. She became a Christian later in life and struggled in vain to accept the fact that God could love her and forgive her for what she had done. This struggle ended when she experienced a powerful and unexpected vision. In this vision she saw herself walking past a university library on the campus in our town. As she passed she looked inside and saw Jesus standing there beckoning her to come in. She was struck with panic since she feared the library was full of books categorizing all of her sins. She knew if she entered, her life would be exposed; and she would suffer the most humiliating experience imaginable as the horror of her past life was reviewed. But because she was also afraid not to respond to Jesus, she felt trapped and entered. He greeted her putting His arm around her terrified frame and took her to the stacks of books. And sure enough just as she had expected, the books opened to contain a record of all her sins in vivid detail. As Jesus opened each book and turned every page, He smiled and pointed out a red cross stamped on each and every leaf. His words to her were, "Why did you wait so long to come in? I have so wanted to show this to you." Today this woman is studying for the ministry, but more importantly she is free. God really does love us even in the face of our fear that He will reject us. It is so sad that many of His people not only resist His grace but also withhold it from others. The single most important tool of a peacemaker is his or her experience of inner peace freeing him to show that grace to others.

The fourth characteristic of a gracious father is that he is not overly passive toward his son. At the proper time he ran to meet him, spared no expense in celebrating with him, and became shameless in his joy. If we put ourselves in the place of the prodigal son for a moment, we might feel the father's absence is a sign he does not care. When we are in trouble, we may feel God is absent and does not care if He does not answer our prayers for deliverance. We must resist concluding that God does not care just because He seems distant in our time of trouble, refusing to come to our aid *in our distant land*. It is our trouble that may need to do its work in our lives before we can fully understand and experience God's radical grace and the freedom that it brings. If the father had helped the son be successful in the distant land, the son could still be there.

When the father sees his son coming, he releases his joy and rushes to make contact with him. We too must not be stingy with our joy in accepting and affirming others when they make themselves vulnerable. After all we are the Body of Christ, and as such we are the feet that run to show grace with joy over those who repent.

In the early years of my ministry I had a home office, and when I was there, I made it clear that I was always free to be interrupted by my kids. I made sacrifices to go to the recitals, ball games, school plays, and anywhere else my kids were involved. I did this not because it was my duty, but because I delighted in them and their stuff. I skipped board meetings at my church for ball games where my son didn't even get to play because I wanted to be there when he did get to play. The absent, disinterested, self-absorbed father is a major problem in our culture. As dads we need to get involved without being possessive. Getting my project in on time at work is important to me, but showing up at the ball game may be even more important.

When I feel abused or neglected by God, I remind myself of Moses, Jesus, Paul, and Peter. Their circumstances gave them little reason to conclude that God was there or doing anything for them. Yet they intrigue me because they knew God's love and favor in spite of their failures and circumstances. They recount their stories in Scripture by not hiding any of the shameful details while expressing confidence in God's love for them.

John Gottman has written an insightful book entitled *Why Marriages Succeed or Fail.* In it he claims he can predict the success of a marriage by listening to how the husband tells the story of the history of the relationship. In those cases where the husband was positive, the marriages worked. In those cases where the husband's story was one of despair and regret with a consistent negative tone, he observed that the marriages tended to fail. A gracious father looks past the negative and sees the positive in his penitent son. Relationships that work call for attitudes that easily forgive, look past failures, and celebrate the best in others.

I am struck by the fact that the father in this story has not one word to say about the son's former behavior. The past is gone, forgotten, and unimportant to the father. A grand party is thrown to celebrate the son's return and to help the son also forget his past. Forgetting past failures can be a problem for those of us who are challenged by a religious spirit. Every time we are called to move forward with confidence, we remember our past failures and the disqualifying effect they threaten to have on our lives. It is not insignificant that Satan is called the *"accuser of the brethren"* (Rev. 12:10) as he constantly reminds us we are not OK. It is for this reason big parties are very important to those who repent. God's people need to make a big deal of repentance, not just because of the joy they feel, but also because of the message it sends to the returning sons and daughters as well as others who may live in fear of rejection.

So what do we learn from the father? We learn that God's grace is extreme, unexpected, and extravagant. We learn that radical repentance is met with radical grace.

Lessons from the Older Brother (Luke 15:25–32)

The older brother is an important part of the story because of the contrast that he represents to the father. It is the older brother's character that underscores the important point of the parable—radical grace.

Jesus had a problem with religious people, as did Paul. If the parables of the lost sheep and the lost coin earlier in Luke 15 conclude with a subtle finger pointing to the religious leaders of Jesus' day, the parable of the lost son ends with a punch in their face. The controversy surrounding Jesus centered on His conflicts with the religious establishment of His day. The religious leaders were especially critical of Jesus' close contact with sinners and His disregard for some of Israel's sacred traditions. Jesus' harshest words were addressed to the religious community for its lack or grace, glaring hypocrisy, and stubborn spiritual elitism.

Paul, following Jesus' example, singled out the same religious spirit in his criticisms. In Galatians 1:6–9 he says, *"I am amazed that you are so quickly deserting Him who called you by the grace of Christ, for a different gospel; which is {really} not another; only there are some who are disturbing you, and want to distort the gospel of Christ. But even though we, or an angel from heaven, should preach to you a gospel contrary to that which we have preached to you, let him be accursed. As we have said before, so I say again now, if any man is preaching to you a gospel contrary to that which you received, let him be accursed."* This new *"contrary"* gospel was the religious spirit evident in the prodigal's older brother. Sadly this religious spirit is in each of us and dominates many Christian groups. We must sense God's resistance to this religious spirit is just as strong as His resistance to pagan immorality and witchcraft.

Radical grace in action brings out the true nature of the Father (God) and the true nature of the older brother (the religious spirit). The older brother was not interested when the prodigal demanded his inheritance, when he played the fool, when he was crushed with pain, when he came to his senses, when he committed himself to come home, and when he humbled himself before his father. But when the father's grace was radically displayed on the prodigal, the older brother's interest is aroused and he explodes with anger. This was Jesus' experience. He got attention when He blessed the "wrong people."

Three Characteristics of a Religious Spirit

Three characteristics of a religious spirit are seen in the life of the older brother. I use the word religious spirit to describe the human religious impulse that takes an outward form of godliness but knows little of the real kingdom of God and its radical grace. It takes pleasure in sacrifice but not mercy (Hos.6:6). It exalts human effort and moral merit. It promotes pride, a judgmental attitude, and shame. It is not good news but death. God resists the religious spirit; it is contrary to the message of the cross. It may play lip service to grace, but the fine print is full of law.

The first mark of a religious spirit is that it is a score keeping spirit. Note the older son's words, *"Look! For so many years I have been serving (slaving away) you, and I have never (emphatic) neglected a command of yours"* in verse 29. The older son was very aware of his own self-sacrifice in slaving away for his father. He was angry that the prodigal (who was delinquent) got this special blessing and he (who was disciplined) did not. He felt entitled to a reward because of his faithfulness. He was keeping score. He knew all about the prodigal's vices and his own virtues. Isn't it interesting to observe how easy it is to see the sins of others and not our own spiritual need for grace? Did not Jesus make a point of this in the Sermon on the Mount where He spoke of those who saw a speck in the eye of others while neglecting the beam in their own eye

105

(Matt.7:3–5). I sometimes get the impression that the first spiritual gift every Christian receives is the gift of discerning sin *in the lives of others*.

The following characteristics are the mark of a score keeping spirit: Christian obedience is a burden carried only because of the reward it earns or the judgment it prevents. It is identified by the sour dill pickle look—where Christian faith is carried like a head cold. Worship is not a free expression of thanksgiving but an investment credit. People feel good for having gone to church even though they brought nothing to the service and left with nothing but a relieved conscience or critique. As a young boy I can remember wondering if heaven was going to be like a very long church service—not the most exciting prospect for a sixteen-year-old boy looking for excitement.

One pastor I know refused to allow the use of any cooking additives that had fermented materials because it could be linked to alcohol, which he felt was forbidden to "real" disciples of Christ. He took great pride in suffering for Jesus and made it quite clear that if others were really serious about the faith they would do the same. "If I suffer when obeying, then all others better suffer in the same way." The score keeping spirit is preoccupied with a childish form of fairness. Our culture demands free choice in all areas of life until people get in trouble, and then they want to claim they were in bondage to some syndrome and are therefore 1) not liable for the consequences of their choices and 2) entitled to special rescue. We too often hear of people who get away with murder because somewhere in their past they suffered parental abuse or ethnic rage. Who hasn't suffered abuse and who doesn't have rage? Who is there that can't claim membership in some kind of "victim" group? This cultural dynamic has spilled over into the church. I often sense we want credit for our moral discipline and a free pass for our moral failures. How often have we felt we didn't deserve this or that trial in life since we have been faithful to Christ and sacrificially served others? Religious pride of superficial good works and bitterness toward those who are not bound to the rules often accompanies a score keeping spirit. We feel abused if we don't get special credit for our suffering under religious rules.

Another characteristic of a score keeping spirit is the power game that is a part of much of the religious system. It is a game where traditions and laws administered by insecure leaders with sagging self-esteem and inflated egos control other people. Contrary to popular opinion, there is no virtue in religious discipline in and of itself. God's purpose is not simply to get people to be more involved in religion, which is too often an institution of human manipulation and moral pride. Rather it is God's purpose to bring people to the light of who they are without Christ, who they have become in Christ, and whose image they bear as God's children.

There are few things better than healthy religion and few things worse than unhealthy religion. One counselor characterized much of Christian culture as preoccupied with "self" (it's all about me!). It has little room for weakness in those who call themselves disciples of Christ. It believes that if it works to make me feel better, it must be of God. While I would not say these are the only ways to characterize church people, I must admit that his critique hits a nerve. There is a lot going on in some Christian circles (as in many religious institutions) that can be characterized as narcissism and pragmatism.

The second mark of the religious spirit is that it is not only a score-keeping spirit but also a separatist spirit. The older brother became angry and *"was not willing to go in,"* according to verse 28. The pride of the religious spirit often comes from being aloof with respect to others who do not share a religious spirit. In most cases these types wind up devouring one another in their preoccupation with witch hunting. "I am more separated than you." One group I know refused to have fellowship with any believer who had any tie to the Billy Graham evangelistic association because "Graham" had a Catholic priest on the platform of one of his crusades in the 1950s. Such attitudes sound very much like the Pharisee spirit of Jesus' day.

Jesus' comfort with human weakness and failure was notorious. This should not be understood as permissiveness or disregard for the holiness of God. Jesus had much to say about judgment and the consequences of prideful rebellion. But Jesus refused to identify Himself with the religious separatists within the Jewish religion. In seeking to defend the holiness of God, these religious leaders had smothered the mercy and grace of God. To be sure there was no party thrown for the prodigal son while in the distant land. But once he had come home, the fellowship, intimacy, and celebration was in order.

The apostle Paul makes this point in 2 Corinthians 2:5–11 when he notes that Satan might take advantage of those with a shameful past by keeping them in shame. Radical forgiveness expressed in a grand celebration serves to break the shame. I have known leaders who have failed in ministry. In some cases their stories have been tragic not because they did not repent of their sins, but because they were never fully forgiven by the Christian community. They were left on their own and became cynical of the church and even of the faith. To make matters worse the Christian church would often say, "This response just exposed their true colors." Perhaps their response exposed something else—something in the church that threw them under the bus. Could following the example of the father in throwing a party have prevented this? Could this be an example of Satan's schemes warned by Paul in 2 Corinthians? The Christian community bears some responsibility to follow the example of the father rather than the older brother. Peacemaking means forgiving in a grand way.

The third mark of the religious spirit is that it is a superficial spirit. Listen again to verses 30–32: *"But when this son of yours came, who has devoured your wealth with harlots, you killed the fattened calf for him."* And he said to him, *"My child, you have always been with me, and all that is mine is yours. But we had to be merry and rejoice, for this brother of yours was dead and has begun to live, and was lost and has been found."* The play on words here is dramatic – *"this son of yours," "this brother of yours."* Not only does the older brother refuse fellowship with the younger brother physically, but also he can't identify with him spiritually. He does not see his own need for grace. He does not see that he is in a different "distant land" (pride) and also needs to repent. According to the older brother, his life is under control. It is manageable. He keeps sins superficial—dress, food, recreation, attendance at meetings, so he never has to repent. He does not see the pride, jealousy, and preoccupation with self that condemns him as much as the foolish living of his younger brother. He can't understand the dynamics of shame, repentance, grace, and joy. The gospel party is not for him. The story of the Pharisee and the Publican strikes at the same issue. *"I thank Thee that I am not like ... this Publican"* contrasted with *"God be merciful to me a sinner"* (Lk.18:10–14). There are many modern day Pharisees who declare war on abortion, pornography, and homosexuality while ignoring or even encouraging elitism, racism, materialism, consumerism, overzealous nationalism, and self-serving individualism. As I said earlier popular evangelical subculture tends to be narcissistic, superficial, pragmatic, and perfectionist. It too often is "all about me." It is satisfied to simply "look good" and offer simplistic solutions to complex problems. If it works to bring bigger numbers, raise money, or help me cash in on the American dream, it must be of God. It tends to kill its wounded. It has lost its saltiness. It has failed to bear the fruit of the Spirit, which is the life of grace energized by deep gratitude to God.

What are the lessons we should learn from the older brother? First, we must identify the religious spirit in our lives and deal with it harshly. The first step to avoid the religious spirit is to identify the false gospel spirit in our own lives. We all try to make a safe place for ourselves without repentance. We want to make life manageable. But

God resists the proud and gives grace to the humble, and we need to do the same in our churches. We need to make it safe to repent and safe to be honest in our struggles. We need to realize that life is often messy and full of inconsistencies that need to be honestly addressed, not hidden or swept away.

We can also overreact in our response to legalism. There is no virtue in fleeing a religious spirit of legalism only to be proud of our lawlessness. The early church at Corinth apparently had this problem of overreacting to rules. I remember speaking before a large congregation in Texas where I had the honor of staying in the home of one of the church leaders. He took great pride in showing me his ample supply of liquor with the comment, "We don't tolerate legalism around here." I was impressed with his liberty but not his humility or maturity.

This story ends with the father and the prodigal in close fellowship while the older brother is self-excluded. The father and the prodigal share this one common characteristic: they traffic in radical grace. It also can be said of them that they are peacemakers.

Paul was at one time in his life an older brother (one of the Pharisees) and later became a prodigal son *("wretched man that I am")*. It is not surprising that he is the champion of grace. Paul's letter to the Romans outlines steps to a changed life that parallel the story of the prodigal son. Paul talks about radical despair, hopelessness, and insecurity in oneself before God in Romans 1–3. He then talks about radical grace in the cross through faith in Christ in chapters 4–5. From there he addresses radical bonding with Jesus as master in chapter 6–11. He concludes with radical ministry to others in the power of the Holy Spirit in chapters 12–16. King David is identified as a "man after God's own heart" not because he was sinless, for he was guilty of adultery and murder for starters. He was a Godly man because, like the prodigal, he was broken by his sin.

A point to ponder

There is no virtue in being proud
of our adherence to
or our freedom from the law.

Early in Luke 15 we read Jesus' words to "*take up our cross and follow Me*." He then proceeds to share parables about compassion for sinners and grace toward the penitent. Could it be that we take up our cross and follow Him when we move away from score keeping, separation, and superficiality? Could it be that we have fellowship with Him as we learn to humbly repent and receive forgiveness for ourselves and in our fellowship with others? In Christ, God does not count our sins as demerits nor does He count our virtues as merits. He just sees His Son and so do we if we are following Him. Grace means brokenness and is as important as obedience. If we find peace in this life, it will be through our experience of grace encountered on the far side of the brokenness of true repentance. It is there that we become peacemakers. Peacemaking is not so much a technique as it is a spirit that is contagious as it demonstrates grace and inner peace in relationships.

Steps to Application

1. Look at the story of the Prodigal Son again and list as many contrasting characteristics between the father and the older brother as you can.

2. Reflecting on a challenging relationship in your life at this time, write a report of how you have responded, are responding, or plan to respond. Then critique it based on the contents of this chapter.

3. After identifying specific attitudes and behaviors in your life that look like the older brother's spirit, design and commit yourself to an equally specific corrective response.

4. Ask someone close to you to give you feedback about your behavior and attitude toward someone who has hurt you. Ask your friend to help you make a plan to reinforce or correct things you don't like about your attitude or behavior.

Questions for Discussion

1. Can you give examples from your life that illustrate the spirit of the father?

2. Can you give examples from your experience that illustrate the spirit of the older brother?

3. What do you think it might take for the older brother to see the light?

4. How would you summarize this chapter?

5. Are there parts of this chapter with which you disagree? Why?

Section III

Grace and Fruitfulness

The story of two Lenders: Grateful and Selfish

*Authentic grace will find expression
in human relationships.*

Jack played softball three nights a week and then afterward went barhopping with his old high school buddies until early in the morning. During these outings he was frequently seen with other women even though he was married. He would then come home to his wife and two daughters expecting to find them happy campers. When confronted by his wife, he would tearfully promise to change; but for two years he continued to repeat his delinquent behavior. She asks, "What can I do? I love him and want our marriage to work, but I have had it. He is driving me crazy, and I am not going to forgive him again." Should she continue the cycle of forbearance? In this case there are two challenges: What does God want to do in the life of the wife, and what does God want to do in the life of the husband? In this case the husband has some serious problems that no wife should ever have to put up with. But it is not the husband that is our focus here. The wife's challenge will be considered as we turn to Matthew eighteen—the story of two masters. Before this young wife will be qualified to minister to her wayward husband, she will have to deal with some issues in her own life.

As we come to this final story in our lessons on grace and peacemaking, we will consider the relationship between grace and fruitfulness. More specifically we will ask the question: How should the experience of the radical grace of God in Christ affect our walk—especially our interpersonal relationships?

A point to ponder

Christianity that does not start with the individual does not start. Christianity that ends with the individual ends.

I hope I have made it clear—what happens to us is not so critical as how we respond to what happens to us. It is not our sin or the sins of others that disturb our peace so much as our response to our sin and the sin of others.

Forgiveness and mercy toward those who have offended us is an important emphasis in Christian teaching. But this teaching raises all kinds of questions. What are the limits of forgiveness? Should we allow ourselves to be manipulated by those who give no sign of repentance or change? Does love lead us to keep forgiving in this context? What would Jesus say?

Matthew 18

"21 Then Peter came to Jesus and asked, "Lord, how many times shall I forgive my brother when he sins against me? Up to seven times?" 22 Jesus answered, "I tell you, not seven times, but seventy times seven. 23 "Therefore, the kingdom of heaven is like a king who wanted to settle accounts with his servants. 24 As he began the settlement, a man who owed him ten thousand talents was brought to him. 25 Since he was not able to pay, the master ordered that he and his wife and his children and all that he had be sold to repay the debt. 26 "The servant fell on his knees before him. 'Be patient with me,' he begged, 'and I will pay back everything.' 27 The servant's master took pity on him, canceled the debt and let him go. 28 "But when that servant went out, he found one of his fellow servants who owed him a hundred denarii. He grabbed him and began to choke him. 'Pay back what you owe me!' he demanded. 29 "His fellow servant fell to his knees and begged him, 'Be patient with me, and I will pay you back.' 30 "But he refused. Instead, he went off and had the man thrown into prison until he could pay the debt. 31 When the other servants saw what had happened, they were greatly distressed and went and told their master everything that had happened. 32 "Then the master called the servant in. 'You wicked servant,' he said, 'I canceled all that debt of yours because you begged me to. 33 Shouldn't you have had mercy on your fellow servant just as I had on you?' 34 In anger his master turned him over to the jailers to be tortured, until he should pay back all he owed. 35 "This is how my heavenly Father will treat each of you unless you forgive your brother from your heart."

When we examine the occasion for this parable, we recognize that Jesus wants to make one powerful point about grace. *God's grace is inexhaustible.* It is capable of enduring innumerable offenses without ever being used up. To use Paul's phrase, *"Where sin abounds, grace does all the more abound"* (Rom.5:20).

The disciples knew they should forgive sinners, but their question here had to do with the limits of forgiveness—"how many times do we forgive...?" Jesus teaches them that there should be great reservoirs of forgiveness in them that would extend way beyond what they might imagine. We might say Jesus calls His followers to endless patience and grace. But we ask, "Is this kind of grace really loving? Doesn't tolerance have limits?" Yes, it does. It does not take a lot of experience in life to realize it is possible to contribute to the delinquency of others by allowing them to continue destructive behavior without consequences. Jesus is not telling us a wife should keep receiving her husband after repeatedly abusing his daughter and then simply saying, "I'm sorry." Jesus is not suggesting an alcoholic should be excused for the twenty-third "I'm sorry" when it is known he or she will continue to abuse themselves again.

This parable is addressed to the heart of the disciples, not to the delinquency of the offender. This is critical in understanding the point of the story and in not distorting its application. After repeated rounds of stuffing their bitterness, the disciples want to settle the score. If the disciples' concern was for the sinner, Jesus may have told a different story. It is helpful to make a distinction at this point. The distinctions are between on the one hand my taking personal offense, and on the other hand love of my neighbor. It may be necessary for me to exercise "tough love" if my motive is genuine selfless concern for my neighbor. But if in withholding forgiveness I am motivated by a personal sense of bitterness and vengefulness, then I am without excuse and cannot hide my selfishness behind "tough love," "justice," or "God's will."

There are a number of other observations that can be made from this parable. First, God's grace toward us should motivate a gracious response to others, especially those who have offended or wronged us. If there is a central theme to Christian ethics, it is love for the neighbor—even the enemy—in response to God's love for us.

Second, it is possible to receive grace and yet not be gracious. We know this to be a fact not only from this parable but also from our personal experience, and most dramatically from the repeated exhortations to graciousness in the Epistles. Paul, for example, in Ephesians 4:32 tells believers to *"be kind to one another, tender-hearted, forgiving each other, just as God in Christ also has forgiven you."* This exhortation would be unnecessary if Christians were *consistently* gracious.

Third, when we are not gracious, we will suffer the same treatment from others. The master (who represents God) in this story seems to be lacking in grace by the end of the parable. When he hears of his servant's lack of grace, the master withdraws his grace. Is this not hypocritical? Let's consider another way of looking at this story. Is it possible that the master simply turns the ungrateful steward over to the natural consequences of his life choices? Those who are ungrateful will ultimately be treated the same way by their fellow man. Is it not possible that while God may forgive us, if we do not forgive others, He will allow us to suffer at the hands of our fellow man until we learn the lesson? In this context the master may not be acting out of vengefulness but out of compassion. What we see here may be an example of "loving discipline" not hypocritical rage.

The verb form of the Greek word translated *"torturers"* is used of illness (Matt.4:24; 8:6) or spiritual anguish of life (resulting from bitterness). In other words, if we who are forgiven refuse to forgive, we can expect the discipline of God and the natural consequences of 1) bitterness and 2) harsh treatment to extract what is due from our lives. Jesus' teaching in the Sermon on the Mount makes the same point: *"Do not judge lest you be judged yourselves. For in the way you judge, you will be judged; and by your standard of measure, it shall be measured to you"* (Matt.7:1–2). While these words might apply to God's treatment of the ungrateful, they may just as likely apply to the way other people will treat those who show no grace or mercy. In other words, what goes around in social relationships comes around. We reap what we sow.

A point to ponder

Grace is suffering the loss of an outstanding debt.

This parable invites some important questions: What is the relationship between grace and obedience? What is the role of exhortation to faithfulness under the New Covenant? What are we to make of the many warnings given in the New Testament Epistles to those who disobey? How does radical grace produce the fruit of faithfulness, obedience, service, ministry, worship, etc.

As we give our attention to the gracious master in Matthew 18, we will see that grace involves yielding our personal rights. It may involve forgiving an outstanding debt and covering the loss ourselves. We will also look at the way grace motivates people to faithfulness. As we compare these two lenders, we will see how God responds to those who do not live gracious lives. When is discipline an act of grace, and how should believers confront a person from a posture of grace? Let's contrast these two lenders:

The Grateful Master	*The Ungrateful Servant*
Had a just claim	Had a just claim
Listened to pleas for mercy	Would not listen to pleas for mercy
Was merciful	Was harsh
Did not insist on strict justice	Insisted on strict justice
Turned the ungrateful servant loose to suffer the consequences of his chosen life	Is left to suffer the consequences of his chosen life

Jesus wants to make one powerful point. In light of the greatness of God's forgiveness, we should be more than willing to forgive one another. Graciousness expressed in forgiveness is at the heart of spiritual fruitfulness. The fruit we are to bear as Christ's disciples is first and foremost graciousness in the face of personal injustice. Returning to our opening illustration the abused wife in this case needs to exercise some tough love toward her delinquent husband but only after she has been willing to suffer injustice in the service of forgiveness. We are qualified to discipline only those we love and are willing to forgive over and over.

Take the following personal inventory. Choose between the two statements "a" or "b." Which best describes your understanding of grace?

1.

(a) When either my friends or I have been hurt, I want those responsible to be punished.

(b) When I have been hurt, I see an opportunity to show grace or grow in grace.

2.

(a) I often become bitter when I am treated poorly.

(b) When I suffer unjustly, my first response is to listen, learn, and respond from a position of being loved by God if not by man.

3.

(a) I expect to learn from my mistakes and the misdeeds of others. I may miss out on something I "deserved," but I don't want to miss out on the lesson to be learned.

(b) I seem to have a hard time learning from my mistakes.

4.

(a) I have a hard time absorbing the loss of blessings that should have been mine.

(b) I realize a big part of forgiving is the willingness to suffer the loss of what I could have, would have, or should have received.

5.

(a) When I see sin in another's life, my first response is to confront them or talk about them.

(b) My first response to sin in someone else's life is to assure them of God's love and then look for opportunities to help them see life in a bigger picture.

6.

(a) I do not believe there is ever any reason to expect anything less than perfect obedience to any and all specific commands of Scripture.

(b) I realize moral decisions in life may call for "damage control" where I choose between the lesser of two evils.

7.

(a) Anyone who is a member of a Christian church and commits a sin should be confronted and challenged to repent or leave the church.
(b) I realize we are often called to forbear with each other in our immaturity, ignorance, or irresponsibility.

8.

(a) When my rights are violated, I see an opportunity for the development or demonstration of character.
(b) When my rights are violated, I demand justice—period!

9.

(a) I believe Christians should look for opportunities to display grace and truth together wherever possible.
(b) I believe Christians are called to promote what is right and that means we follow and enforce the rules.

10.

(a) I hate to see guilty people get off the hook.
(b) I want people to profit from their mistakes, but I experience no joy in seeing people suffer.

11.

(a) I look for opportunities to display God's grace, especially when it is not expected.
(b) I find it hard to forgive and forget.

NOTE:

The (a) statements represent an ungrateful spirit while the (b) statements represent a more gracious posture in all but #3,8,9,11 where it is just the reverse.

Chapter 8
The Grateful Master's Cross

Step #5 to Peace with God: Empathy

Peacemakers must be able to empathize with others.

I received the following letter from a woman who had suffered considerable injustice in a difficult marriage and messy divorce:

"I am writing to share with you the final chapter in the long process of becoming free of anger and bitterness brought on by my inability to forgive. For years, as you know, I have struggled, living with the pain of a broken marriage and the legal fights that followed. Sometimes friends who took the time to listen to try to understand some of the details of my struggles eased the pain. I prayed and they prayed for me to have this anger just go away, but it persisted. I would remind myself of God's promise, "Vengeance is mine; I will repay," but that somehow didn't really ease my anger and pain at all. I felt guilty knowing that I would only feel better when the people who hurt me had to pay for what they did. It also didn't help to be reminded that my anger and inability to forgive was only hurting myself, that I was unpleasant to be around, and that I even looked angry and bitter. I was stuck.

It was Good Friday in 1990, and I was sitting in the courtroom alone waiting for the attorneys to return with the judge from his chambers. Because of a series of legal technicalities, I had been frustrated in my attempts to get justice. I was left with deep-rooted bitterness. This was year seven for me, and I was still fighting and angry, although sometimes pretending not to be, even trying to fool myself.

As I sat alone in the courtroom, God hit me over the head with a simple truth. As a Christian I knew what Good Friday was all about. But in my preoccupation with the hurt and injustice done to me, I had forgotten that God not only shared my pain from being mistreated but also bore the injustice of my mistreatment of Him and others. The rays of light shining through the window that Good Friday began to penetrate my heart. Who was I to demand justice when Christ, who was more a victim than I would ever be, willingly died for me so that one day I could stand before God forgiven? As I sat there waiting for the judge to return, my anger began to lift. My emotions went from bitterness and anxiety to embarrassment. My inability to forgive what was done to me struck me as insignificant compared to what I had been forgiven. This is one Good Friday that I will never forget because it changed my life."

Our response to injustice and to others in the face of their failure is a powerful witness to the grace and peace imbedded in the Gospel. Matthew 18 depicts God as the gracious master who forgives. Again, let me summarize the teaching of Jesus' parable. According to Jesus' parable we are expected to put ourselves in the place of the forgiven servant and extend the same grace to others. This gracious response is so important that if we fail to respond graciously, God will see that we are treated (by others) without grace so that we might become empathetic.

Grace, not Fear or Guilt, should Motivate Christian Living.

Love and grace are to motivate our response to life's injustices in ways that glorify Christ. Fear, guilt, anger, and promise of reward will also motivate to action, but the greatest motivation for the heart is love. People are often afraid that grace will not motivate heartfelt obedience, but it is the most effective way to reach deeply into the soul.

As a pastor I am committed to using love and grace, not guilt and fear, in inspiring ministry. If grace does not bring results, then I will live without results. Ministry motivated by guilt, fear, or material reward may look good on the outside and may work in the short term; but it is not worth the sacrifice of the integrity of the gospel. We frequently would tell people in our services when the offering basket was passed, don't feel obligated to give unless you have been a recipient of God's grace. And then if you are a Christian, give as an act of worship; not with the expectation God will "bless you if you do" and "get you if you don't." This is a worship service not a market.

Paul states the issue clearly in Ephesians 4:32: *"And be kind to one another, tender-hearted, forgiving each other, just as God in Christ also has forgiven you."* 1 John 4:19 reads, *"We love because He first loved us."* It is clear—our faithfulness is a response to God's grace. We could cite many other Scriptures that make the same point (Rom.12:1–2, 15:7, and Ti.2:11–12).

A point to ponder

Spiritual fruit bearing is most simply a Godly response to circumstances.

Paul Repeats the Message of Jesus.

I remind you again of the structure of Paul's letters illustrating the point of Jesus' parable. After explaining the mercy of God in chapters 1–11 of Romans, Paul exhorts and encourages his readers to live lives of obedience showing grace to each other in service of God. Most of the Epistles in our New Testament follow this same sequence. First there is a reminder of God's grace toward us followed by an exhortation to respond in kind as we relate to others. It is important to recognize that like Jesus, Paul is addressing genuine believers who have been forgiven yet are not forgiving others. The point of Jesus' parable of the two lenders is applicable to Christians today. Many who are true disciples of Jesus still have unresolved issues of forgiveness in human relationships.

Grace is not Inconsistent with Moral Standards.

Moral standards among Christians are not inconsistent with radical grace. Anyone who reads the New Testament will recognize it is full of exhortations to holy living. Some breaches of conduct and doctrine are viewed as more serious than others. Certain types of conduct in the Corinthian church of Paul's day warranted harsh discipline while other offenses did not receive such treatment. Open sexual immorality, for example, brought harsher treatment while a sense of spiritual elitism did not. The expected level of outward obedience seems to be related to the level of maturity and responsibility of the Christian. Elders, especially teachers, were held to a higher standard of conduct and doctrinal confession than young believers, for example.

Moral discipline is a part of radical grace (See Appendix #3). It must be remembered however that all discipline is to be an expression of love (Heb.12:4–11). If you can't discipline another from a spirit of love, then you are not yet qualified to do the disciplining. Elders in a congregation have the responsibility to exercise church discipline and do so in the context of a New Covenant where ethics are more sophisticated than the superficial demands of the Old Covenant. Under the New Covenant the leading of the Spirit from within replaced the letter of the law from without. While the letter of the law can give us insight into wisdom in matters of discipline, we should not be afraid of following the Spirit of love as we approach each situation. The law can address outward behavior but it takes the Spirit to restore the inner heart. In the complexity of life's challenges there is a need for flexible, Spirit led, wisdom. The law will never be detailed enough to replace a virtuous, mature, shepherd's hand in pastoral care. A nation or a congregation that lacks an installed, inner, spirit of love and only has laws will not fair well. It will too often miss the mark of wisdom and leave a trail of abused and broken relationships rather than restored saints and a healthy community.

Grace does Not Exclude Temporal Consequences of Disobedience.

The New Testament Epistles contain many appeals to obey with warnings about the consequences of disobedience. In Ephesians 4 we have a good example: *"17 So I tell you this, and insist on it in the Lord, that you must no longer live as the Gentiles do, in the futility of their thinking. 18 They are darkened in their understanding and separated from the life of God because of the ignorance that is in them due to the hardening of their hearts. 19 Having lost all sensitivity, they have given themselves over to sensuality so as to indulge in every kind of impurity, with a continual lust for more. 20 You, however, did not come to know Christ that way. 21 Surely you heard of him and were taught in him in accordance with the truth that is in Jesus. 22 You were taught, with regard to your former way of life, to put off your old self, which is being corrupted by its deceitful desires; 23 to be made new in the attitude of your minds; 24 and to put on the new self, created to be like God in true righteousness and holiness."*

Warnings like this and the one found in Galatians 6:7–8 can be unsettling and are often misunderstood. Galatians 6 seems to suggest that "eternal life" is conditioned upon our sowing to the flesh versus the Spirit: *" 7 Do not be deceived: God cannot be mocked. A man reaps what he sows. 8 The one who sows to the flesh, will from the flesh reap corruption; the one who sows to the Spirit, will from the Spirit reap eternal life."* While it is true that sowing to the Spirit can be equated with "faith" that leads to eternal life, the context of this passage (vs.6-7) links it to the way we support and receive the preaching of the Word. If we do not encourage the ministry of the Word, we invite spiritual starvation through a lack of teaching.

Bearing Fruit is a Response to Life's Circumstances.

Jesus uses the analogy of a vine and branch to teach his disciples the dynamic of fruit bearing (Jn.15:1–11). As the disciple, (a branch) responds to the vine (Christ), he will reflect the life of Christ. As I noted in chapter one, Paul describes love in terms of our response to life's circumstances – "*Love is patient, love is kind and is not jealous; love does not brag and is not arrogant, does not act unbecomingly; it does not seek its own, is not provoked, does not take into account a wrong suffered, does not rejoice in unrighteousness, but rejoices with the truth; bears all things, believes all things, hopes all things, endures all things.*" (1 Cor.13:4–7). There is no mention of serving the needs of others. There is no mention of obeying the law of God. There is no mention of feelings of compassion for the lost. What we have instead are a number of expressions suggesting patience and kindness (grace) in the face of personal insults and experiences of injustice. In short Paul is saying that love is a gracious response to the injustices of life. Are we to conclude that love does not involve self-sacrificing service to the needs of others? No. But we must sense that a gracious response to the injustices of life is at the core of the greatest commandment.

From Vengeance to Blessing

The apostle Peter was not known for grace and peace until the Spirit of Jesus was installed in his life. The converted Peter wrote a letter that was completely out of character with his old life and a powerful testimony to the Spirit of Christ imbedded in his soul. 1 Peter 3:8–9 "*8 to sum up, all of you be harmonious, sympathetic, brotherly, kindhearted, and humble in spirit; 9 not returning evil for evil or insult for insult, but giving a blessing instead; for you were called for the very purpose that you might inherit a blessing.*" Our baptismal covenant involves a commitment to die to our selves. God expects us to take our baptism seriously. With the death of self (ego) there is freedom not only to replace vengeance with forgiveness but also to bring a blessing to those who hurt us.

On Monday morning, October 2, 2006, a gunman entered a one-room Amish school in Nickel Mines, Pennsylvania. In front of twenty-five horrified pupils thirty-two-year-old Charles Roberts ordered the boys and the teacher to leave. After tying the legs of the ten remaining girls, Roberts prepared to shoot them execution style with an automatic rifle and four hundred rounds of ammunition that he brought for the task. The oldest hostage, a thirteen-year-old, begged Roberts to "shoot me first and let the little ones go." Refusing her offer, he opened fire on all of them killing five and leaving the others critically wounded. He then shot himself as police stormed the building. Why would anyone do such a thing? Roberts told the children before he opened fire "I'm angry at God for taking my little daughter."

Following the tragic shooting reporters from throughout the world invaded Lancaster County, PA to cover the story. However in the hours and days following the shooting a different and unexpected story developed. In the midst of their grief over this shocking loss the Amish community didn't cast blame, they didn't point fingers, and they didn't hold a press conference with attorneys at their side. Instead they reached out with grace and compassion toward the killer's family. The afternoon of the shooting an Amish grandfather of one of the girls who was killed expressed forgiveness toward the killer's family. That same day Amish neighbors visited the Roberts' family to comfort them in their sorrow and pain. Later that week the Roberts family was invited to the funeral of one of the Amish girls who had been killed, and at Charles Roberts' funeral Amish mourners outnumbered the non-Amish.

It's ironic that the killer was tormented for nine years by the premature death of his young daughter. He never forgave God for her death. Yet after he cold-bloodedly shot 10 innocent Amish schoolgirls, the Amish almost immediately showed compassion toward his family. In a world at war and in a society that often points fingers and blames others this reaction was unheard of. Many reporters and interested followers of the story asked, "How could they forgive such a terrible, unprovoked act of violence against innocent lives?" Eventually the Amish community set up a charitable fund for the killer's family as they continued to grieve for not only their loss but also for the loss that Robert's family experienced.

Within a week of the murders Amish forgiveness was a central theme in more than 2,400 news stories around the world. The Washington Post, The New York Times, USA Today, Newsweek, NBC Nightly News, CBS Morning News, Larry King Live, Fox News, Oprah, and dozens of other media outlets heralded the forgiving Amish. From the Khaleej Times (United Arab Emirates) to Australian television, international media were commenting on Amish forgiveness. Three weeks after the shooting, "Amish forgiveness" had appeared in 2,900 news stories worldwide and on 534,000 web sites.

The Amish culture closely follows the teachings of Jesus who taught his followers to forgive one another, to place the needs of others before themselves, and to rest in the knowledge that God is still in control and can bring good out of any situation. Love and compassion toward others is to be life's theme. Vengeance and revenge is to be left to God. This is peacemaking in action.

Grace and Forgiveness are at the Heart of the Great Commandment.

Forgiveness is to be extended even when there is less than an appropriate change of behavior. In Colossians 3:13 we are told to forgive each other as God has in Christ forgiven us. This must mean that we be *willing* to forgive before there is a complete change of heart and life. God's grace sets the context for our forgiveness in that he forgives us before he reforms us. He forgives sinners who are still in need of repeated repentance.

Forgiveness does not mean however that loving correction is inappropriate. Let's revisit the real-life situation that I mentioned at the beginning of Section III. This was a situation that called for forgiveness and also tough love between a wife and her unfaithful husband. I counseled this young wife to tell her husband she loved him and valued his life and their marriage too much to let this continue. If he continued to act as though he were not married, she was going to change the locks on the house; and he would not be able to return until he found a way to demonstrate he was going to take his life and marriage seriously. As long as he chose to act as a single person, she was also going to respect his decision and treat him as unmarried. This is not an act of bitterness or vengeance. It is an act of mature and responsible love. How long should this delinquent husband be locked out? He should be locked out until his wife was convinced he had changed! How long would that take? She will decide. What can and must he do to convince her? He must do whatever it takes for as long as it takes. But it should be noted that she could not take this step without first forgiving him. Her motive had to come from care for him and the marriage not from bitterness, vengeance, and self-protection. Divorce may be an option but only as an act of loving care not self-interest.

Grace calls forth Assurance before Confrontation.

The question of when to comfort and when to confront is almost always difficult to answer. I often tell people if they want to keep their friends, avoid confronting them on how they spend their money, raise their kids, or conduct their spare time. Even when they ask for advice, be reluctant to give it. There are few people who will receive critical commentary on these sensitive areas of life until they are really desperate. What can we do to help (confront and correct) others? We can provide an example of how to deal with money, raise our kids, and spend our time. Let the

Holy Spirit take it from there. There are times for bold open confrontation but generally expect to comfort others before confronting them. And when we must confront, do so with humility and sensitivity.

Our comforting of others should never be an endorsement of poor behavior but should involve empathy with their feelings of pain and fear. Strong feelings should first be acknowledged with a response of empathetic feelings not dispassionate ideas. Save the insights for later. Remember the way Paul writes his letters. He starts with affirmation, comfort, and encouragement even when he knows harsh correction will follow. He confronts, corrects, and exhorts only after affirming. We win the right to confront after we have convinced others that our intentions are motivated by love and our perspective is governed by God's grace.

When my youngest son was eight years old, I took him to see the movie *Hoosiers*. I thought he would enjoy the experience, but I was wrong. He fussed and squirmed through the entire film making the experience unpleasant for the whole family. On the way home he continued to fuss and cry. I had had it. I made sacrifices to give him a good time, and he did nothing but make everyone miserable. I told him I was very disappointed in his behavior, and we were not going to do this again. He cried even louder. After two or three more minutes of disgust, I suddenly realized how selfish I had been. I had decided what my son was going to enjoy, and when he didn't respond the way I expected, I was angry. When I realized this, I turned to my son and said, "I'm sorry. I was not thinking of you and what you would enjoy. It was unfair for me to expect you to respond to my plans for you. If this happened to me, I would be upset just like you are." Immediately my son stopped crying. For the first time in the "conversation," his Dad was listening to him. When he felt understood, his mood changed.

I have often remembered this experience when ministering to people who are emotionally upset. It is important to affirm the authenticity and legitimacy of feelings before addressing other issues. When I am emotionally upset, I may want someone to fix the situation; but I first and foremost want someone to share my situation emotionally. I want someone to affirm my feelings of anxiety, frustration, fear, or anger. I want to know that I am not alone in my pain, frustration, and disappointment. The following acronym is a guide that I keep in mind.

L isten to the concerns
O verlook faults
V alue strengths
E mpathize with pain

People will forget what you say, people may forget what you do, but people will never forget how you made them feel. If you want to make someone's day, love him by empathizing with his pain. I am frequently frustrated in playing golf. On more than one occasion I have wanted to throw my club after I made a poor shot. I usually control myself so I won't look like an idiot, but inside I am really frustrated. It seldom helps to be playing with someone who though well intended is bent on correcting my bad swing and my bad response. One day while golfing with a friend, I made a terrible shot. I was boiling inside. My friend, Tom took his club and hit the ground as hard as he could in frustration for me. He did the very thing I wanted to do. When he did it, I felt something special. He shared my pain to the extent it became his pain. After that I was less inclined to react in frustration. Sensing that I was not alone in my feelings was a feeling more powerful than the feeling of frustration. When we feel we are not alone in our fears, anger, frustrations, or pain, we move toward peace. Tom was a peacemaker that day. If we cannot confront or correct out of empathetic love, we need to work on our own stuff before we try to help others. This is a common theme in Scripture (Matt.7:1-5; Rom.8:17-18).

Damage Control

The need for damage control is often overlooked in pastoral ministry even though it has a sound biblical basis. The classic example is seen in the divorce laws of Deuteronomy 24. Jesus makes it clear, *"Because of your hardness of heart Moses permitted you to divorce your wives; but from the beginning it has not been this way."* (Matt.19:8). Divorce is not God's will, but because of a hardness of heart, divorce is permitted and controlled. In the ancient culture of Palestine women needed social security that came from being a part of a male-led household. If they were not cared for in a marriage or home, they needed some form of social protocol placing them in the care of another family. If a husband put his wife out of his home, she needed a formal statement freeing her from his family. Divorce provided protection for her. It was necessary given the sinfulness of human nature even though divorce was not a part of God's ideal plan.

We still have hard hearts, and we still need to respect the place of damage control. This is seen in many areas but probably most often in issues surrounding divorce and remarriage. When someone has made repeated mistakes and gone through several marriages, it is often not possible to make everything work according to the book. No one excludes from the church divorced people who are remarried under less than ideal circumstances. There are times when strict adherence to the letter of the law seems at odds with the growth of a person to wholeness. In such cases love may demand that we permit a lesser form of violation of the Scriptural ideal in order to prevent a greater sin. I think of the biblical story of Rahab the harlot who lied to protect the Hebrew spies in Joshua 2. I don't think we should encourage people to lie, but I realize in some situations there are even greater evils than lying, requiring us to exercise some damage control. Moral judgments in this area are challenging and call for pure hearts and sensitivity to Christ's Spirit.

Grace May Call for Forbearance of Some Sins.

The church at Corinth provides a classic negative example of forbearing with sins that should have brought harsh discipline. The Corinthian church was passing judgment on issues that called for forbearance and forbearing issues that called for harsh discipline. Christians were being discriminated against because of their gifts or social contacts while open sexual immorality was celebrated.

Paul's letters are full of pleas for forbearance. His letters are addressed to churches with sin problems, but note that Paul does not excommunicate, condemn, or otherwise reject all sinning believers. There are certain situations where discipline was required and issued, but it was used sparingly. Forbearance was more often Paul's response. By forbearance I mean a willingness to tolerate or put up with offenses, selfish acts, and immaturity. Romans 2:4 speaks of the forbearance which leads to repentance, and in Romans 3:25 we read of God's *"forbearance of sins previously committed."* In Ephesians 4:2 Paul exhorts believers *"with all humility and gentleness, with patience, showing forbearance to one another in love."* Forbearance is not needed except when there are offenses, insensitivity, and other sins that *continue* to be a problem.

I met a college student who grew up in an abusive home. As she entered adult life, she began to work out a lot of issues of anger toward her parents. Her college roommate grew up in a loving Christian home and did not struggle with some of the same serious issues. The church was appropriately patient with the first girl's struggle and more demanding with the second girl due to their unique backgrounds. Both displayed outbursts of anger that were hurtful to those around them, yet more was expected of one than the other. This is not inappropriate given the special circumstances in each of their lives. In no way does this suggest we "get off the hook" if we have a "victim card" in our hands, but I am saying human conduct is complex and to whom much is given, much more is expected. The corollary is also true. When little is given, less is demanded. We are not all given the same number of talents (Matt.25:14–30). This is one of the reasons it is not wise to compare oneself with others. We each have our own unique burdens to bear and gifts to offer. God will one day do the judging of our hearts and actions according to His infinite and perfect wisdom. In this life we are called to be witnesses for grace more than lawyers or judges of the law.

Because You're Mine, I Walk the Line.

Paul was fully aware that grace could be abused and become an opportunity for the flesh to be active outside the moral law of God. But he also was convinced that when God's love is fully experienced through His grace, it would have a powerful constraining effect on our lives. Johnny Cash's hit song "I Walk the Line" was written as a commentary on the power of love to produce faithfulness: *"I keep a close watch on this heart of mine. I keep my eyes wide open all the time. I keep the ends out for the tie that binds. Because you're mine, I walk the line."* I am reminded of Paul's words in the book of Romans (chapter 6). *"1 What shall we say then? Are we to continue in sin that grace might increase? 2 May it never be! How shall we who died to sin still live in it? 3 Or do you not know that all of us who have been baptized into Christ Jesus have been baptized into His death? ... 8 Now if we have died with Christ, we believe that we shall also live with Him, 9 knowing that Christ, having been raised from the dead, is never to die again; death no longer is master over Him. 10 For the death that He died, He died to sin, once for all; but the life that He lives, He lives to God. 11 Even so consider yourselves to be dead to sin, but alive to God in Christ Jesus."*

Paul realizes if the grace of God is understood as radical, it will lead to the question: What is left to restrain our sinful passions? Paul's answer is significant. He does not appeal to the law or the threat of judgment upon those who fail to keep the law. Rather he draws attention to our identity in union with Christ. *"Because you're mine, I walk the line."* When we grasp the love, grace, and intimate union we have with Christ, we are bound to a new way of living that involves obedience. We must not forget who we are. An effective worship service should among other things remind worshipers who they worship and who they are in Christ.

After being away at college, I came home on Thanksgiving break. While walking down the street of our hometown, I met an elderly man who knew my family and recognized me. As we made casual conversation, he commented on how much my grandparents had inspired him with their work ethic and integrity. I distinctly recall his words: "You have a great heritage to live up to. We have always expected great things from you." I mention this because of the effect it had on me. I went away from that conversation feeling thankful, proud, and inspired. My family identity brought with it a responsibility as well as a privilege. Have I always lived up to that responsibility? No. But that conversation keeps reminding me of who I am and what is expected of me. It is a compelling reason to walk the line.

We can make two mistakes in our assessment of the gospel. First, we can burden it with what might be called "front-end loading." We can demand moral virtue and behavior up front before the blessings of the gospel can be made available. We can demand that a person clean up their life before they become a Christ follower. The second mistake we can make is to "back-end load" the gospel. We can insist that unless a person is obedient to the moral laws of God, they are not really a part of the Christian family. This leads to a misunderstanding that their faith is not genuine, authentic, or effective in uniting them with Christ until and unless they meet His moral demands. Faithful obedience should be expected from those who receive the grace of God, but it is not always evident or perfect. The New Testament letters were written to genuine believers who were in need of exhortation to faithfulness. Love not fear is the motivation for Christian faithfulness. Peacemaking does not take place without a grateful and graceful heart. *"So show your love for the alien, for you were aliens in the land of Egypt."* (Deut.10:19)

Tips for Application

1. Pray on a daily basis that God would make you sensitive to opportunities to respond to your circumstances in a Godly way.

2. Memorize the acronym and practice it:
   L isten to the concerns
   O verlook faults
   V alue strengths
   E mpathize with pain

3. When you are convicted of some act of sin in your life, take the opportunity to let it lead you to its source (underlying motivation). The grace of God makes it safe to explore deeper motives and longings. It also equips us to make peace with others.

Questions for Discussion

1. What do you believe to be the most common signs of false faith?

2. Why do many Christians continue to be bitter?

3. What are we to make of confessing Christians who have not resolved issues of bitterness in this life?

4. How can "damage control" be applied or abused in areas like sexual ethics, emotional illness, and childhood abuse?

5. How would you summarize this chapter?

6. Are there parts of this chapter with which you disagree? Why?

Chapter 9
Do you want Justice or Peace?

Obstacle #5 to Peace with God: Justice

Peacemakers must be willing to suffer personal injustice.

My parents disciplined me when I was young. I usually deserved any punishment that I received. But it strikes me as significant that of all the specific instances of discipline, I remember the one incident where I was innocent. Like most folks I am sensitive to injustice especially when it impacts me personally. I find that forgiveness for injustices suffered is a universal challenge. Bitterness can stay with us a long time, and it can rob us of inner peace and joy. Bitterness is a poison that eats away at our soul. Until we can forgive, we will not find peace; and we certainly will not be peacemakers. But here is the kicker. So long as we demand justice we will be burdened with bitterness, anxiety, and anger. We can't have peace if we insist on justice for ourselves.

> ### *A point to ponder*
>
> Bitterness is like drinking poison and expecting someone else to die.

I asked an African American friend for advice on how to promote peace in our racially charged culture. His answer was quick, "No justice, no peace." In other words the key to social peace in his view was to demand justice. This advice may be on target in a political dialogue, but it is distinctly different from the point made in the story told by Jesus. The peace coming from grace is not a peace demanding justice. It is a peace without a demand for justice. The most successful champions of social peace in our world were also champions of grace without full justice—Gandhi, Nelson Mandela, Martin Luther King Jr., etc. In the Apostle Peter's first letter (2:11–3:12) he offers a powerful argument for "peacemaking" through gracious suffering with Christ. This is especially significant when you recognize the natural tendency in Peter to want and even demand justice in the face of injustice.

Social justice is important, but the inner peace we need and long for cannot wait for a just world any more than it can wait for just people. I have come to believe that personal inner peace is a key to social justice not visa versa. I also understand grace to be peace without justice. Sadly it is possible to be a recipient of grace but not a dispenser of it. This chapter focuses attention on the second character in the story of two debtors in Matthew 18, and it argues that personal inner peace cannot demand personal justice.

In many ways the ungrateful servant is both the subject and the target of the story in Matthew 18:15–35. He represents the audience to whom Jesus is speaking. We must assume we too are in that audience, and that we all can identify more easily with this ungrateful servant than with the grateful master. What do we learn from his story? How does this story contribute to our understanding and experience of peace with God? And how does this instruct us in peacemaking?

It seems to me the ungrateful servant teaches us at least three things: 1) The inspiration for social reconciliation in our relationships is the grace of God toward us. 2) Forgiveness may require the forfeiture of justice and bearing the loss of what is due us. Demanding justice can be an obstacle to peace. 3) Empathy is so vital to graciousness that God will discipline us until we "get it."

There are six points of tension that challenge us as we seek to learn from the ungrateful servant.

#1 Feeling verses Logic.

In this parable Jesus frames empathy in the context of logic not emotion. For Jesus empathy is a feeling that is based on a logical deduction. The story of the graceless master does not appeal to our emotions. It is an appeal to our sense of logic and reason. If we understand and appreciate the grace of God, we should logically be eager to express that same treatment to our fellowman. The fact that both Jesus and Paul appeal to this logic is significant. When we actually understand and deeply believe the radical grace of God and how much we have been forgiven, we will or should make the connection in our response to others. By extending grace to others, we become peacemakers. Both Jesus and Paul suggest that the root issues are knowledge, reason, and faith. Biblical exhortations to forgive are often put in the context of teaching about God's grace and the challenge to walk by faith.

We should deeply feel God's love and grace, but Jesus' teaching in Matthew 18 appeals to the minds of His audience not just their feelings. He is asking us to reason with Him and come to our senses. We cannot overstate the importance of the "renewed mind" (Rom.12:1–2). Much of the teaching of Jesus and the Apostles is an appeal to our intellectual responsibility—a sense of logic. They expect us to shape our behavior by our thinking, perceptions, and reasoning not by our emotions or impulses. This is not to be confused with an academic faith or a passionless life that is lived only "out of our head." But it does tell us that robust faith must be intellectually convincing. As children of Romanticism (a form of the Enlightenment) we tend to notarize everything with "feeling", as though the only reality is what we passionately feel.

#2 Accepting verses Alleviating Suffering

Forgiveness almost always involves suffering if we are asked to forfeit a sense of personal justice. We may have to give up an impulse to seek revenge, preserve our reputation, and hold on to our material possessions. To forgive a debt means to absorb the losses. If I keep holding on to my rights after I have expressed forgiveness, I will become disappointed or bitter. I must accept the losses and move on. In this respect grace is costly. If Christians are to experience and express peace, they must find a way to accept the losses coming from personal injustice. It is only when we "bear the loss" or give up what is justly ours that we will be free from the bitterness that blocks peace. Jesus spoke of bearing a cross as a part of following Him. He absorbed the loss of His rights when He became sin for us. His peace was not without suffering injustice, and so it will be for us as we follow Him, for we are not greater than our Master.

The ungrateful servant refused to give up what was due him because he failed to respond to the grace that had been shown to him by one who did give up what was due. In a broken unjust world we will have many opportunities to forgive debts as people refuse to give us what we deserve. I might go so far to say that when we continue hanging on and demanding our rights, we will lose more than our rights; we will lose the peace we wrongly thought our rights would bring. Bitterness is like taking poison and expecting someone else to die. Those who refuse to forgive reject the freedom and peace of God's kingdom. When we die to ourselves, we die to a spirit demanding justice for self. When we are willing to forfeit justice for ourselves, we can no longer be intimidated by the world. We are no longer vulnerable to an imperfect world that can and certainly will abuse our rights. We will have a peace the world cannot give or take away, a peace that surpasses worldly understanding. And most important we will know Christ as we share his suffering. There is a price for peace. It is the same price we pay for following Jesus. Peace makers are first peace seekers who because of God's mercy present themselves as living sacrifices.

A point to ponder

A servant's role in life is to be an
accompanist to someone else's solo.

Jesus set the standard. He gave up his rights by dying for those who sinned against Him. When we are offended, we are asked to be gracious and forgive without vengeance or bitterness. This means that we are willing to suffer loss like Jesus, as a part of the *"fellowship of His suffering"* (Phil.3:10).

Absorbing the loss of justice, personal rights, dreams, and temporal hopes requires faith and grace at a deep level; but it is absolutely essential to peace. This becomes especially hard when the loss involves our children, our reputation, our vocation, our health, our church family, and our expectations of God. But the peace God offers is designed just for such circumstances.

Peace is not possible when we lose touch with God's grace or the Cross. When we refuse to forgive others as we have been forgiven and insist on justice in response to the wrongs done to us, we indicate that we have forgotten the gospel story. The grace that produces peace is the grace that shapes our posture toward those who have disappointed or hurt us. Social justice is an important part of a political peace plan for a fallen world, but it will not bring the kind of personal peace that Jesus offers and we desire. Peace dependent on our experience of justice in life will be very vulnerable. Our peace will be an uneasy and anxious existence wondering when the next foot will drop. Peace without justice is one of the more radical elements of the gospel. It is a distinct characteristic of a disciple of Christ. It is one of those areas where Christians are set aside from the world. It is a mystery to those outside the faith, but it should not be a mystery to those inside the fold.

#3 Empathy verses Autonomy

Another issue that keeps us from peace is a lack of empathy. Now we might think that autonomy (independence from others and the circumstances of life) would be more important than empathy in experiencing peace. After all, if we could just not take things so personally we would feel less anger and fear. Isolation is not the path to peace.

My youngest son, David, attended a very large high school where he was honored to be chosen by his classmates as prom king his senior year. This gave special significance to the fact that a year after David left for college we received a phone call from a student at his old high school. We did not know the caller but discerned that he was probably a special education student by the way he spoke. He said he was one of David's friends and asked to speak to him, but we informed him that David would not be back from college until spring. We asked him how he knew David and he replied, "David would eat lunch with me." David had never mentioned this young man, and we would have never known about this relationship had not we received this call. I make two observations from this revelation with respect to our son's life. First, I was impressed by the fact that our son, who was among the most popular students in the school, would have a social circle that included students near the other end of the social pecking order. This told me a lot about our son's character—kindness, sensitivity, and empathy. Second, I could not help but draw a connection between our youngest son's behavior and his personal experience since he had a brother who was profoundly autistic and mentally retarded.

I have not hesitated to tell people how thankful and proud we are of our three children—including our oldest son Daniel. Daniel's autistic condition is profound. He has never spoken a word, and yet he has enabled us to hear things that words could not convey. He has never known us as his parents, and yet he has profoundly influenced our family. He has never been able to express or receive our expressions of love, and yet he has branded into our hearts pictures of the passionate nature of God's love for us in our spiritually autistic condition. The things that are most painful for us often carry a powerful, hidden blessing as they bear the fruit of empathy.

A point to ponder

The Golden Rule can be reduced to one word—EMPATHY.

The Golden Rule

The Golden Rule—do unto others as you would have them do unto you—is the heart of Jesus' ethical teaching and can be reduced to one word—EMPATHY. Empathy is vital to both Christian ethics and spiritual formation. At the heart of the gospel's appeal is empathy, the ability to appreciate God's holiness and our lack thereof, which creates a context whereby we can understand the atoning value of the cross. Empathy enables us to appreciate the transfer of our shame to Christ and God's grace to us. Love calls for empathy. Without empathy there will be little community, caring, and compassion. Emotional, social, and spiritual maturity depend on empathy.

In Tod Lindberg's insightful book, *The Political Teachings of Jesus,* he correctly notes that the Golden Rule is at the heart of the political impulse of Western (especially American) moral and legal thinking. The Golden Rule was a radical teaching in Jesus' day as it still is in many parts of the modern world. The idea that people are equal and deserving of equal treatment may seem strange in societies where men are viewed as "above" women, where masters are superior to slaves, where the rich have rights that the poor do not, where one's skin color or ethnic heritage gives them more power and value than others, and where the educated, gifted, and well-born are more deserving than those who are not. Equality as "liberty and justice for all" may not sound radical to many of us in America today, but it surely was and still is radical in much of the world (past and present).

You have perhaps heard the statement—"There are two types of people in the world, those who are like me and those who should be like me." International relations between our country and culturally different nations provide a mirror into our own empathetically challenged souls. Projecting our cultural values onto others rather than empathizing with those who are different in some way is too common and can lead to foolish decisions. As one network commentator put it in his frustration with political tensions in Israel—"Why can't they all just act like good Christians"? The stereotyping of race (both black and white) is a painful part of world culture, not just America. Socio-economic class, nationality, ethnic origin, and religious affiliation are common dumping grounds for empathetic insensitivities. Sweeping social critiques too often suggest a personal lack of empathy in our lives. Social stereotyping reflects a part of our soul, a part we tend to deny because we don't want to see ourselves as insensitive. The fact is, those of us who lack a deep experience of peace with God are often empathetically challenged.

Toxic Empathy

Does empathy automatically bring peace to our souls? The answer is NO! Empathy is a natural characteristic of healthy humans, but some temperaments are by nature more empathetic than others. For some of us empathy seems automatic while for others is more difficult. The naturally empathetic temperament is quick to sense and share emotional pain almost to a fault. Far from being at peace these folks can be anxious, sleepless, and nervous. Bearing the burdens of others in the power of the Spirit of Christ is a virtue, but when we bear those burdens in the flesh, it can lead to empathy fatigue. This is not the path to peace. Healthy boundaries are related to our "big picture" of the Kingdom of God and are vital to Christian empathy. We are reminded that Christ and Paul knew when to deeply care and when to shake the dust from their feet and move on.

Empathy can help us experience God's grace, but it in itself is not the key to peace. Empathy can be a curse to those who are bound and overwhelmed by it. It can feel like a prison chaining us to all the pain around us until we become emotionally overloaded and spent. This toxic empathy fatigue is emotionally disturbing and not what God is calling us to embrace. The challenge is to know how to care and not to care. That is to say, we need to easily share the burdens of others and at the same time have emotional and spiritual boundaries. Caring that causes us to lose our own peace, perspective, and power is not healthy.

Do You Have a Healthy Empathy?

1. Can you sense the common human aspirations in the lives of those who disagree with you politically, socially, and religiously?

2. How quickly do you respond to the discipline of life's circumstances?

3. Is there an emotional empathetic element in your meditation on the cross of Christ?

4. Do you absorb the pain of those around you without knowing how or having a place to release it?

5. Can you deeply care for the pain of others and yet enjoy life and sleep at night?

6. It is much easier to empathize with those who have not personally hurt us, but the real test comes with those who have hurt us. How do you handle these cases?

Spiritual Sociopaths

What happens when empathy is rarely experienced or not present at all? Perhaps the most disturbing element in any community is the sociopath. A sociopath suffers from a profound lack of empathy. Sociopathic individuals do not care for others simply because they do not identify with them. They live lives of psychological dissociation. They feel pain and joy in their own lives but have little emotional sense of what others may feel in response to the sociopath's selfish behavior. We all have elements of emotional dissociation in our lives. Even the most empathetic personality types can be strangely removed from others who have hurt them or who are "different" in some way.

The graceless master's lack of empathy is a trail-head to a path leading deep into his forgetful, irrational, and faithless soul. We are looking at a person who acts like a spiritual sociopath. He seems to have completely forgotten or misunderstood the way that was shown to him by the Gracious Master. Grace had not impacted him strongly enough to ward off the pain of personal injustice. It is likely that the graceless servant's rage eclipsed any remembrance of his own misconduct and the grace that came in response. He of course is not alone. We are far too prone to throw a pity party or pride parade at the drop of a hat. When we are treated unfairly, we can feel pity for ourselves and use it to excuse our bitterness, revenge, and withdrawal. When we accomplish something good, we pat ourselves on the back and look for ways to showcase our image to those whose acceptance we see as the source of our security, significance, and serenity. Such reactions are natural but selfish. When we are not prepared for personal injury in a fallen world, we can easily be derailed by it. When we forget our tendency to face personal injustice with a lack of empathy, we will reap the effects in our behavior. How are we to overcome this sociopathic inclination? In a word the answer is GRACE.

At the root of the problem is an inadequate experience and handling of grace. Radical grace, if not deeply experienced, can simply be an excuse for the flesh. But when we know the depth of our own spiritual depravity and the extent to which God in Christ has affirmed us, we will sacrificially serve those around us.

A point to ponder

**When you get kicked under the bus,
you may find yourself in a crowd
and with Jesus.**

4. Universal Grace verses the Grace of God in Christ.

We forgive because we were first forgiven in Christ. Grace is not cheap but we are not the ones paying the cost. Grace costs us nothing because its cost was born by Christ. If we miss this point we misunderstand a critical part of grace.

Let me illustrate this point of tension with a fictitious story borrowed from the late Dr. James Kennedy. Let's say that in the midst of a public address where I am speaking, two policemen come through the back door and ask me to come downtown with them. You are in the audience and are completely baffled by the incident. The next day you read in the paper that I had been arrested for multiple murders. You are shocked but assured there has been a mistake. After a short trial you read that I confessed to the crimes and are sentenced to death. Being a compassionate Christian your heart goes out to me. You decide you are going to approach the judge and offer to take my punishment for me that I might go free. When the judge hears your request, he denies it but offers this alternative option. The court would not accept your life for mine, but it would accept the life of your only daughter. You are distraught but muster up the faith and courage to accept the court's proposal. The judge tells you that if you accept this option, you must perform the execution of your daughter. As she is strapped to the electric chair, your heart sinks. You close your eyes and pull the switch knowing your daughter's innocent life is snuffed out while my guilty life is spared. I am set free and several weeks pass. You are in a restaurant, and I walk in but do not recognize you. I sit in the booth next to you with my friend, and you overhear our conversation. My friend asks me how I could be pardoned from the crimes I had committed. Your heart breaks as you hear my reply. I say, "The court must have looked at my overall record and decided there were a lot of good things I had done in my life, and there were a lot of people I could have killed or abused that I didn't. And after it was all said and done, the court just decided to be gracious." Overhearing this you shake your head wondering how I could have forgotten about your pain and the sacrifice of the innocent life of your daughter. Sound familiar? Is this not the Gospel story?

A child was asked to recite her favorite Bible verse, and she quoted John 3:16 with a slight lapse of memory: "For God so loved the world that He gave His only *forgotten* Son that whosoever believeth in Him should not perish but have everlasting life." We must never forget the cost of God's grace and the injustice He endured for us as we are called to live lives of grace and gratitude.

A young man who came to my office tearfully confessed that he had been unfaithful to his wife. He was broken, full of shame, and remorse for what he had done. I informed him that the bad news, his adultery, was just the tip of the iceberg. Like the prodigal son his sin was more serious than adultery. Adultery was a symptom of a more basic rebellious independence from God. His story also illustrates good news because he was now in a position to know God and himself, as he had not before. The radical grace of God through Christ was more than sufficient to cover his shame. He need not hide from God in his shame but should run to Him as his refuge and strength. Let tears of shame be turned to tears of thankfulness not for what sin has done to God and those He loves, but for what God has done to sin. Where sin abounds, grace does all the more abound (Rom.5:20). But this grace is not cheap. It comes at the cost of Christ's atoning work on the cross. There is a need for deep sorrow for sin but we are not to be left in despair or hopelessness. Our failures, when put on the cross of Christ, are trophies of grace that should bring great joy and peace to us as they draw us to worship God.

5. Radical Grace verses Law and Grace

For some of us the correct Biblical understanding of God's grace is not freedom from the law but rather power to obey the law. We preach grace, but in the fine print of our message we see law. We make it clear that we are saved by grace, but that the grace that saves will and must obey. In the end if there is not practiced righteousness, there is no positional (justifying) righteousness. This is a grave error in my view. If law is even a small part of the covenant, it effectively trumps grace and makes the contract a legalistic one—no good works = no salvation.

I have spoken of spiritual formation in terms of 1) knowing yourself, 2) accepting yourself, 3) forgetting yourself, and 4) giving yourself. The depth of our need and the radical nature of God's grace are the keys to the first two points. If we only know our need, we may be over-whelmed and depressed. If we only know of God's mercy, we may use it as an excuse for the flesh. If we do not die to ourselves, we will find it hard to be gracious with others. And if we do not "show up" for work in God's Kingdom, we may lose the joy of participation in the Body of Christ, which is our designed purpose and holy calling.

We may understandably think, *"where grace abounds, sin will all the more abound."* It is tempting to conclude selfishness is so powerful that without firm laws it cannot be controlled. The first part of the statement is correct; the selfish gene in us is very strong. The second part is naïve. The flesh is controlled not by law but by grace and death. The law might reap superficial positive results, but it will not bring greater spiritual maturity or inner, long-term change. Teaching too much grace is not the cause for sin. Too little grace, superficial grace, or distorted grace can be a problem but not too much grace. When we have a superficial sense of God's love and our own depravity, we are dangerous to one another and ourselves. The last two points of spiritual formation (involving the expression of grace) are based upon "the first two points" (the experiencing of grace).

5. Suffering Personal Injustice verses Working for Social Justice

What are we to make of the Biblical Prophets who speak so strongly and clearly about doing justice for the weak, poor, powerless, and forgotten people of this world. Are they to be ignored in light of Jesus teaching in this parable? Some critical distinctions must be made at this point. First, in this parable, Jesus is speaking of those who are unable to pay their debts but humble, broken, and willing to pay if they could. In a sense they have a conscience and are penitent. How would the parable have been used if, let's say, the individuals were able but unwilling to pay, if they were thieves or selfish, greedy, irresponsible, conmen? I suspect the parable would have brought a different message. We remember the parable of the talents where the lazy servant was harshly penalized (Matt.25:14-30).

We are not asked to simply forgive those who have abused us (or others) and show no signs of repentance. Nor are we to demand that everyone else who has been unjustly treated "get over it", "take the loss", and "forgive." We are asked to respond with gracious love. To many the proper response will be to forgive and take the loss. To others it may mean loving discipline, "tough love", and a call for reparations. In each case however we who have been treated graciously by God are challenged to be motivated by that act to be gracious and loving to others. We must be willing to suffer the loss of justice for ourselves unless love demands that we serve the good of another through discipline.

Peacemakers must Shed the Chains that Bind them.

A heartbroken father shared his pain with me over broken relationships with his adult children. Before he came to faith in Christ, he had been through multiple marriages and was now facing the pent up anger of the children from those broken relationships. He wanted to be reconciled, but it seemed one of the children was determined to be sure that he hurt as much as she did. He was made vulnerable and imprisoned by the guilt of earlier years of delinquent fathering, and she knew how to pull his chain to activate the shame and guilt in his life. This experience of being yanked around by an emotional chain is not uncommon, but it is so unnecessary.

What did this father need? Repentance from past behavior would certainly be called for. A strategy for rebuilding bridges with his children might be in order. It would be good to show love until the children realized that their father had changed. But before any of this would be productive, there would have to be freedom from the shame and guilt that chained the father to the bitterness of his children. As long as those chains were attached, they would be used to torture both sides of this painful relationship. A deep experience of radical grace is the door to freedom from the chains that others use to manipulate us and that we use to manipulate others. The chains come off when grace is installed in our lives.

Folks who know the grace of God in Christ do not have to manipulate others to find peace nor do they have to yield to the manipulative ploys of those seeking peace from them. If we are to be peacemakers, we must be free from manipulation. The chains must come off.

So how should this father respond to his daughter when he is free? First, he should expect and maintain a relaxed attitude when the angry manipulative attacks come his way. He should be prepared to respond to his daughter with understanding and empathy but without yielding to her attempt to add to his guilt and pain. He should act as though he knows how to care and when to shake the dust off his feet and let his daughter's anger fly past his heart knowing that she will not be helped so long as she can keep getting to him. Loving his daughter means not dancing with her in this childish game of blame and shame.

Peacemakers know when to care and when not to care. They know how to forget about themselves because they sense by faith they are fully accepted in Christ. They are also free to show up and give themselves to the healing ways of God's Kingdom in loving those around them. They do not confuse love with surrender of control to anyone but the Spirit of Christ. They remember that a part of Jesus' power was seen in the simple fact that he refused to manipulate or be manipulated because he did not have to.

6. The Judgment of Believers verses "No Condemnation" of Believers.

How will believers be judged? 1 Corinthians 3:12–15 offers a challenge to radical grace. "*Now if any man builds on the foundation* (Christ) *with gold, silver, precious stones, wood, hay, straw, each man's work will become evident; for the day will show it, because it is to be revealed with fire; and the fire itself will test the quality of each man's work. If any man's work, which he has built upon it remains, he shall receive a reward. If any man's work is burned up, he shall suffer loss; but he himself shall be saved, yet so as through fire.*" How is this to be understood in light of the believer's freedom from condemnation? (Notice John 5:24 "*Truly, truly, I say to you, he who hears My word, and believes Him who sent Me, has eternal life, and does not come into judgment, but has passed out of death into life.*" Romans 8:1 "*Therefore there is now no condemnation for those who are in Christ Jesus.*") How can heaven be heaven if there is judgment and loss?

152

Here is a possible interpretation (a theory). Could our *"wood, hay, and stubble"* (works of the flesh) be exposed as our loss but to God's praise as we see the full impact of the grace of God working *for* us through the removal of our sins at the cross? Likewise, could our "good works" (gold, silver, precious stones) be trophies of the power of God's Spirit and grace working *through* us? I believe we will worship from both the ashes of our failures and from the fruit of our victories. In this way the judgment is real and so is heaven. When we understand the radical grace of God in Christ, we will realize that forgiveness means joy as our failures are fully exposed along with our fruit.

Note Paul's words in I Corinthians 4:3–6. *"But to me it is a very small thing that I should be examined by you, or by any human court; in fact, I do not even examine myself. I am conscious of nothing against myself, yet I am not by this acquitted; but the one who examines me is the Lord. Therefore do not go on passing judgment before the time, but wait until the Lord comes who will both bring to light the things hidden in the darkness and disclose the motives of men's hearts; and then each man's praise will come to him from God"* It is the disclosure of motives that will constitute this judgment of believers. We will all see just how powerful God's radical grace really is as many of those things that we may have been proud of were really driven by very self-serving motives. This judgment will not condemn us but draw us in awe to the Cross of Christ.

Tips for Application

1. Developing a spirit of gratitude and empathy can come as we answer some simple questions.

   - How would I feel if I were in any of a number of hypothetical negative or positive situations?
   - What have I received that I did not deserve?
   - How might things have been different in my life if God had not been gracious?

- Am I comparing myself with people who have more than I do or less? How can I change this?

2. The next time you face a situation where you have a choice of demanding justice or showing grace, show grace even if it means suffering loss. Then afterwards ask yourself how it felt. How did this affect your sense of peace? Was it worth it?

3. Look at each experience of injustice in your life as an opportunity to: 1) Develop Christ-like character, or 2) Demonstrate Christ-like conduct.

Questions for Discussion

1. What is the relationship of peace to justice?

2. Why do many people not respond well to God's loving discipline?

3. How can "damage control" be applied or abused in areas like sexual ethics, emotional illness, and childhood abuse?

4. How would you summarize this chapter?

5. Are there parts of this chapter with which you disagree? Why?

Conclusion

Can the grace of God in Christ bring peace to broken people in a broken world? Can peace seekers who find such peace make peace through reconciling relationships with others? Those who read this book *Peace Makers* and the one that preceded it, *Peace Seekers,* will be left to answer that question for themselves as they respond to its message of God's grace in Christ.

Carla Faye Tucker was executed on February 3, 1998 for the brutal, drug induced, pickax murders of two innocent victims in 1983. In 1985 while in prison awaiting trial Tucker picked up a Bible, read it, and later recalled, "I didn't know what I was reading, and before I knew it, I was in the middle of my floor on my knees; and I was just asking God to forgive me." While some prison conversions bear little real fruit in either inner peace or outer reconciliation, Tucker's conversion by nearly all who knew her was dramatic. The warden of Texas' Huntsville prison testified that she was a model prisoner and that, after 14 years on death row, she likely had been reformed. On the day of her execution some 1700 protesters gathered to voice their opinion (pro or con) of the state's decision to go forward with the sentence in spite of worldwide appeals from the likes of Pope John Paul II, Newt Gingrich, and Ron Carlson, the brother of one of Tucker's murder victims. Her final words bear witness to a very imperfect person who lived in a very imperfect world and yet found dramatic peace. "Yes sir, I would like to say to all of you—the Thornton family and Jerry Dean's family—that I am so sorry. I hope God will give you peace with this. Baby, I love you. Ron, give Peggy a hug for me. Everybody has been so good to me. I love all of you very much. I am going to be face to face with Jesus now. Warden Baggett, thank all of you so much. You have been so good to me. I love all of you very much. I will see you all when you get there. I will wait for you." After her final words, she licked her lips and, according to witnesses, appeared to be humming softly as she waited for the lethal injection. In Linda Strom's book *Karla Faye Tucker: Set Free* she says, "In my 11 year journey with Karla, it was her joy that captivated me. Her story is the story of a murderer who said "yes" to God." Three weeks before her execution she was interviewed by Larry King on national television. King asked Karla, "Can you explain (your positive up-beat attitude) to me a little bit more? It can't just be God." Karla smiled broadly. "Yes, it can—it's called the joy of the Lord. When you've done something like I've done and you've been forgiven for it and you're loved—that has a way of changing you. I have experienced real love…. I know what it is; I know what forgiveness is, even when I've done something so horrible. I know that, because God forgave me when I accepted what Jesus did on the cross. When I leave here, I'm going to be with Him."

Terry Strom put music to Karla's life in his song, "*I See Jesus In You.*"

> I walked into that place,
> And I could see Him in her face.
> His love came shining through—
> There was nothing I could do...
> But be in awe of You, Lord.
> I see Jesus in you.
> I want to be that way, too.

> All of His glory
> Tells me the story
> That He lives in you.
> There is nothing for us to fear;
> And I know that He is right here.
> And when I'm through livin',
> I know I've been forgiven.
> And He'll take me home with Him

In finding peace she was free and committed to making peace.

"*Grace and peace be unto you.*" With these words the Apostle Paul, himself a prisoner on death row, links two of the greatest benefits of the good news of Jesus. God's grace in Christ through His sacrificial atonement and resurrection from the dead brings to us first, positional (legal) PERFECT PEACE with a holy God, and second, psychological peace in an unholy world. Personal peace is the key to social peace. If we are to be peacemakers socially, we must be peace models spiritually.

In this book I have argued for a position that is dangerous, unpopular, and controversial. I have argued that legal PERFECT PEACE with God through Christ is the foundation for psychological and social peace. I have claimed that one can have peace without living a sinless life or without living in a sinless world but not without embracing radical grace. I have argued that the joy in our worship, the rest in our work, tranquility in our souls, fruitfulness in our ministry, and reconciliation in our relationships come from grace and faith apart from perfect moral discipline and the power of faith to change our circumstances. We can have real peace without justice. This is scandalous but it also is the Gospel.

So how do imperfect people in an imperfect world not only find peace but also make peace? The story of two sisters (Mary and Martha) underscored the importance of bringing a Sabbath rest into our lives. It also revealed an obstacle to peacemaking—busyness. The story of two brothers (the prodigal and the older brother) further challenged us to avoid a religious spirit and repent of our efforts to manage life apart from God. And finally, the story of two debtors (the grateful and graceless) indicates that empathy and discipline are important to a life of peacemaking. Demanding personal justice is an obstacle to being a peacemaker.

Inner peace of the soul is not automatic nor is it easy to acquire for everyone, but the path is simple and it is the key to being a peacemaker. We must understand and embrace with faith the radical, scandalous, and scary grace of God. We must step out and walk in grace, stop striving for peace through our moral merit, and start empathizing with those around us who struggle. Ultimately we must pray that God's Spirit will help open our eyes and discipline us to walk in that grace and peace. Paul's prayer in Ephesians 1 is for all of us:

Ephesians 1:15–23

"15 For this reason I too, having heard of the faith in the Lord Jesus which exists among you, and your love for all the saints, 16 do not cease giving thanks for you, while making mention of you in my prayers; 17 that the God of our Lord Jesus Christ, the Father of glory, may give to you a spirit of wisdom and of revelation in the knowledge of Him. 18 I pray that the eyes of your heart may be enlightened, so that you may know what is the hope of His calling, what are the riches of the glory of His inheritance in the saints, 19 and what is the surpassing greatness of His power toward us who believe. These are in accordance with the working of the strength of His might 20 which He brought about in Christ, when He raised Him from the dead, and seated Him at His right hand in the heavenly {places}, 21 far above all rule and authority and power and dominion, and every name that is named, not only in this age, but also in the one to come. 22 And He put all things in subjection under His feet, and gave Him as head over all things to the church, 23 which is His body, the fullness of Him who fills all in all."

Peace Makers raises many questions some of which will be addressed in the appendices that follow. I am fully aware that the grace of God as I have presented it can be misconstrued and misused to the destruction of our lives. Peter spoke of this when he referred to the letters of Paul, *"speaking in them* (Paul's letters) *of these things, in which are some things hard to understand, which the untaught and unstable distort, as they do also the rest of the Scriptures, to their own destruction."* (2 Pet.3:16). He concludes with, *"but grow in the grace and knowledge of our Lord and Savior Jesus Christ."* (vs. 18). With these words Peter ends his letter using the same theme with which he started in chapter 1 verse 2, *"Grace and peace be multiplied to you in the knowledge of God and of Jesus our Lord;"* It is my prayer that we would each find that peace through a holiness that is not of our own faithfulness or through heaven on earth but through a living faith in a gracious God and a righteous Christ. It is my prayer also that our inner spirit would reflect the deep inner rest that Christ won for us with the result that we would be peacemakers to all who meet us.

Anthony De Mello, a Jesuit priest from India tells us the story of a monk who in his travels once found a precious stone and kept it. One day he met a traveler, and when the monk opened his bag to share his provisions with him, the traveler saw the jewel and asked the monk to give it to him. The monk did so readily. The traveler departed overjoyed with the unexpected gift of the precious stone that was enough to give him wealth and security for the rest of his life. However, a few days later he came back in search of the monk, found him, gave him back the stone, and entreated him, 'Now give me something much more precious than this stone, valuable as it is. Give me that which enabled you to give it to me.'"

May the grace of God in Christ be deeply experienced (by peace seekers) and freely expressed (by peace makers).

Summary

Steps	*Obstacles*
#1 The spirit of brokenness before the holy demands of the moral law of God is vital to spiritual peace.	*#1* A spirit of self-sufficiency and confidence before God and His law will keep us anxious, bitter, or proud.
#2 The spirit of a new operating system based upon Christ's performance not ours must be installed for spiritual peace.	*#2* A spirit of perfectionism inviting us to live under the law of Moses will keep us anxious, bitter, or proud.
#3 The spirit of faith in God must be reflected in our hope in Christ's righteousness *for* us and then *in* and *through* us for spiritual peace.	*#3* A spirit of independence looking for hope in anything and everything but God will keep us anxious, bitter, or proud.
#4 The spirit of Sabbath rest must be installed in our everyday lives for spiritual peace.	*#4* A spirit of busyness confusing the work for God with the will of God will keep us anxious, bitter, or proud.
#5 The spirit of repentance must turn our pain into insight that leads us home for spiritual peace.	*#5* A spirit of religion that is scorekeeping, separatist, and superficial will keep us anxious, bitter, or proud.
#6 The spirit of empathy must remind us of the grace that has been shown to us and now needs to be shown by us for spiritual peace.	*#6* A spirit of justice, demanding our rights, will keep us anxious, bitter, or proud.

Appendix #1

Questions about Law and Grace:

There are a number of specific questions that repeatedly appear in any serious discussion of God's grace. Some of the most common questions make up this appendix.

1. *In what sense is the law terminated?*

The law is terminated as a covenant of works with the power to reward and condemn on the basis of obedience. The Law of Moses continues to be a true though superficial expression of God's eternal moral character. As such, it has an abiding value as a moral guide for all people.

John Calvin referred to three uses of the law. It was to restrain sin among all people. It was to convict sinners and drive them to Christ. It was to guide the believer in his walk with God. These three uses are all valid. The question that must be answered is, "In what sense is the Mosaic *Covenant of law* binding on the Christian?"

The basic references that speak of the termination of the law Covenant:

> **Romans 10:4** *"For Christ is the end of the law for righteousness to everyone who believes."*

The word *"end"* could mean "epitome" but is best understood as "termination" in this passage. Christ's example is the perfect expression of the heart of the law. But Christ's crucifixion tells us that the law as a covenant or contract with God's people is finished.

> **Colossians 2:14** *"Having cancelled out the certificate of debt consisting of decrees against us and which was hostile to us; and He has taken it out of the way, having nailed it to the cross."*
> **2 Corinthians 3:11** *"For if that which fades away (vs.7 "the ministry of death, in letters engraved on stones") was with glory, much more that which remains is in glory."*

Ephesians 2:15 *"By abolishing in His flesh the enmity, which is the Law of commandments contained in ordinances."*

Galatians 3:19 *"Why the Law then? It was added because of transgressions, having been ordained through angels by the agency of a mediator, until the seed should come to whom the promise had been made."*

Christ redeemed believers from under the law.

Galatians 4:5 *"In order that He might redeem those who were under the Law."*

1 Corinthians 9:20 *"Though not being myself under the Law."*

Christ freed believers from the Old Covenant.

Galatians 5:1–6 *"It was for freedom that Christ set us free; therefore keep standing firm and do not be subject again to a yoke of slavery. Behold I, Paul, say to you that if you receive circumcision, Christ will be of no benefit to you. And I testify again to every man who receives circumcision, that he is under obligation to keep the whole Law."*

1 Corinthians 6:12 *"All things are lawful for me, but not all things are profitable. All things are lawful for me, but I will not be mastered by anything."*

Christ removed believers out from under the law.

Galatians 4:21–31 *"Tell me, you who want to be under law, do you not listen to the law? ---* "So then, brethren, we are not children of a bondwoman, but of the free woman."*

Galatians 5:18 *"But if you are led by the Spirit, you are not under the Law."*

Romans 6:14 *"For sin shall not be master over you, for you are not under law, but under grace."*

Christ rendered believers dead to the law as a means of achieving righteousness.

> **Romans 7:1,4,6** *"The law has jurisdiction over a person as long as he lives?" "You were made to die to the Law through the body of Christ," "But now we have been released from the Law, having died to that by which we were bound."*
>
> **Romans 10:4** *"For Christ is the end of the law for righteousness to everyone who believes."*
>
> **Galatians 2:19** *"For through the Law I died to the Law, that I might live to God."*

Christ set aside the law by replacing it with a different (higher) standard.

> **Hebrews 7:12** *"For when the priesthood is changed, of necessity there takes place a change of law also."*

2. In what sense did Christ come to fulfill the law and not to abolish it?

Christ came to fulfill all the demands of the law: 1) living a life of perfect love, 2) and providing a "once for all" sacrifice for sin at the cross. He then ushered in a New Covenant through His blood having fulfilled all that the law demanded.

> **Matthew 5:17** *"Do not think that I came to abolish the Law or the Prophets; I did not come to abolish, but to fulfill."*

"Nowhere does Paul say that Christians are to "do" the law, and nowhere does he suggest that anyone but Christ can "fulfill" the law. "Doing" the law refers to that daily obedience to all the commandments that was required of the Israelites. "Fulfilling" the law, on the other hand, denoted complete satisfaction of the law's demands that comes only through a Christian's identification with Christ (Rom.8:4)." Douglas J. Moo, *The Law, the Gospel, and the Modern Christian*, Zondervan, p359

3. How should Christians relate to the law?

Those under the law need to be liberated from the law.

> **Romans 3:19–20**, *"Now we know that whatever the Law says, it speaks to those who are under the Law, that every mouth may be closed, and all the world may become accountable to God; because by the works of the Law no flesh will be justified in His sight; for through the Law comes the knowledge of sin."*
> **Romans 6:14**, *"... you are not under law, but under grace."*
> **Romans 7:4–6**, *"You were made to die to the Law through the body of Christ," "But now we have been released from the Law, having died to that by which we were bound."*

Those above the law need to be broken by the law.

> **Romans 7:9–10**, *"And I was once alive apart from the Law; but when the commandment came, sin became alive, and I died; and this commandment, which was to result in life, proved to result in death for me;"*
> **Galatians 3:12**, *"However the Law is not of faith; on the contrary, 'He who practices them shall live by them.' Christ redeemed us from the curse of the Law, having become a curse for us . . ."*
> **Romans 7:18–24**, *"For I know that nothing good dwells in me, that is, in my flesh; for the wishing is present in me, but the doing of the good is not. For the good that I wish, I do not do; but I practice the very evil that I do not wish... . Wretched man that I am! Who will set me free from the body of this death?"*

Those free from the Law of Moses are guided by the law of Christ (love).

> **Romans 7:6**, *"But now we have been released from the Law, having died to that by which we were bound, so that we serve in newness of the Spirit and not in oldness of the letter.*

Galatians 5:13, *"you were called to freedom, brethren; only do not turn your freedom into an opportunity for the flesh, but through love serve one another."*
1 Corinthians 9:20–21, *"to the Jews I became as a Jew, that I might win Jews; to those who are under the Law, as under the Law, through not being myself under the Law, that I might win those who are under the Law; to those who are without law, as without law, though not being without the law of God but under the law of Christ,"*

4. How does the law prepare us for the gospel?

First, the law was designed to excite an appetite within people for a Savior. This appetite is aroused by a deep awareness of our sin and our inability to correct that sinful condition through self-discipline.

Second, the law would help people identify the future Messiah. Messiah would be the one who fulfilled the law's demands. He would do this for God's people and therefore the law was completed or fulfilled by Christ for them. *"Do not think that I came to abolish the Law or the Prophets; I did not come to abolish, but to fulfill."* (Matt.5:17). This fulfillment in Christ is what Paul had in mind when he wrote, *"For Christ is the end of the law for righteousness to everyone who believes"*(Rom.10:4).

Third, the law, with its detailed sacrificial system, prepared Israel to understand the cross of Christ. The law foreshadowed things to come (Heb.8:5, 9:23, 10:1; Col.2:17), most specifically a Christ who would be a substitutionary sacrifice.

5. Shouldn't we balance law and grace in presenting the whole counsel of God?

Law and grace do not need to be balanced with each other. But their relationship must be properly understood. The law is to be used lawfully, that is in keeping with the purpose of the law. There is an important place for moral law—it is to lead us to Christ, show us God's character, and convict us when we are sinning. The law can no longer condemn us or promise us a blessing for obedience. As a covenant of works it is finished.

When the law (as a covenant) and grace are superficially combined, the law tends to nullify grace. Too often we try to preach the message of grace while holding to the law covenant. Those who hear such a mixed message are confused when they hear grace but feel law.

6. What would life under law and under grace look like for Old Testament believers?

The Old Testament believer's faith in the promise of God would be the basis of his gracious acceptance by God (Rom.4; Gal.3:6–7). The Law of Moses guided the believer's life in the Old Testament demonstrating to the believer his weakness and foreshadowing better things to come. The Old Testament believer demonstrated his faith by observing the covenant with its system of offerings for sin that were a shadow of the Cross of Christ to come.

When the gospel came, it would be good news to the Old Testament believer in that it freed him from the condemnation of the law. The Cross would bring his old nature to death with Christ (consequently rendering him dead to the Mosaic Law system) (Rom.6). It called him to follow a higher law (the law of Christ) in a new and better way (the power of the Spirit through faith). The Mosaic Law would still be respected as holy and spiritual (in that it came from God) but it would be outdated as a covenant by Christ. To revert to the old law and its system of dependence upon the flesh was a great threat to the free manifestation of the Spirit in obedience to the law of Christ.

By way of contrast the wrong attitude of the Old Testament unbeliever or physical Israel would receive the Mosaic law as an opportunity for the flesh to focus on *self justification* through meritorious works apart from faith (Jn.5:45).

The gospel was a stumbling block to the Old Testament unbeliever. It insulted the efforts of his flesh by rendering them worthless. It robbed his flesh of its power and pride by doing away with the Mosaic Law as an active functioning promise of meritorious rewards.

7. What is legalism?

Legalism is a fleshly attitude, which conforms to a code for the purpose of exalting self and gaining merit with God, rather than glorifying God because of who He is and what He has done. A legalistic posture under the Law of Moses would be one that obeys the commandments in order to be identified as a part of the covenant community that would be blessed by God through obedience (Pharisees). The correct attitude would respond to the law in obedience out of reverence for God and for His glory (David). A legalistic attitude under grace can be illustrated by the man who would read the Bible, pray, and do ministry every day in order to: 1) gain God's favor for doing good and 2) gain self-respect and praise among men for being a good Christian. The correct attitude can be seen in the man who prays faithfully for his brother because of a personal experience of God's grace and because of love for the brother. This is contrasted with "law," which encourages the flesh to view behavior as an investment rather than a response to grace.

Another way of looking at legalism is to see it as a preoccupation with the law rather than with Christ. A legalistic life is a life that is law guided rather than Spirit guided.

8. Will grace lead to lawless license and careless conduct?

Grace may not prevent irresponsible behavior as in ancient Corinth, but its intention is to encourage freely chosen virtue. Paul seems to argue in Romans 6 and 7 that it is law, not grace, exciting the flesh to sin. The law is an appeal to the flesh (Rom.8:3, 7:18–25; Heb.7:18). When the question

"*Are we to continue in sin that grace may increase?*" is addressed by Paul in Romans 6, he responds with an appeal to the believer's new identity in Christ. "*How shall we who died to sin still live in it?*" (Rom.6:2). It is interesting to note that Paul does not appeal to the threat of condemnation found in the law.

When Paul writes to the Corinthian church to correct its license, he does not appeal to the warnings found in the law but reminds them of who they once were and who they now are in Christ. "*And such were some of you; but you were washed, but you were sanctified, but you were justified in the name of the Lord Jesus Christ, and in the Spirit of our God*" (1 Cor.6:11). He is saying, in essence, "be true to your new self." When believers misuse grace, it is because they have not really experienced grace at a deep level. In such a case, more grace is needed not less.

9. Does grace really constrain sin, or does it just comfort the sinner?

Grace, when it is fully and correctly understood, will both comfort and constrain the believer. It will assure God's children that in spite of their failures they are and remain reconciled to God and are at peace with Him. It will also constrain the believer's conduct (2 Cor.5:14).

It is hard to fight with someone when we sense they love us. The most powerful motivator in life is love. People will do the most heroic deeds in response to its influence. While it is true that fear and guilt are also powerful motivators, the conduct resulting from fear and guilt does not come from the noblest part of our soul. The faithfulness resulting from love is the faithfulness reflecting God's nature and ours as the bearer of His image. Paul was constrained by God's love not by fear of the law.

10. *Isn't obedience to the law part of saving faith?*

Obedience should normally result from true faith, but faithfulness to the law is not inseparable from true faith. It is possible to have saving faith and yet be disobedient to the moral law of God. If obedience is part of true faith, then we would be like the Pharisees of Jesus' day, judging one another's relationship with God on the basis of conformity to moral performance. James reminds us that if we violate the law at any point, no matter how small, we are guilty of all (Jas.2:10). It is not hard to see that we are quickly in deep trouble when we are under the law. Every letter in the New Testament was written to Christians who were disobedient in one-way or another. Yet these congregations were still addressed as though they were saints.

11. *Can Christ be Savior without functioning as Lord or master in every area of my life?*

This question can be expressed in several ways. How is the Christian community to view a person who professes to believe in Christ as their Savior from the penalty of sin and yet lives a life that is outwardly unchanged and worldly? If a person persists in sinful practices (lying, stealing, sexual misconduct, hatred, coveting, etc.) after professing to be a Christian, should the Christian community recognize them as true believers; or should they be viewed as false believers who have deceived themselves? When people are encouraged to trust Christ, should repentance from sinful deeds be required in order to be saved; or is just repentance from false beliefs about Christ necessary?

Christ is Lord (objectively) no matter what we confess. He is Lord (subjectively) when we actively submit to Him at various points in our experience. Few people can say they are perfectly submitted to Christ as Lord at all times and in every area of life. When someone confesses faith in Christ and shows no interest in following Him, we have reason to question the depth or voracity of their confession. Many people make empty confessions that fall short of true faith (Matt.7:21–23).

Three basic truths need to be respected: 1. Salvation is by grace through faith apart from human merit. It is possible to have true saving faith and yet go to one's grave with unresolved moral conflicts in life. It is possible to have true saving faith and look (outwardly at times) like a non-Christian. 2. True faith is a deep commitment of one's life. It is not a superficial confession of words. 3. True saving faith always bears fruit, at least inwardly (new birth) and often outwardly (changed conduct).

Calling on Christ to save from the penalty of sin is confessing and submitting to Christ as Master or Lord of at least one very important area of life. Saving faith submits to Christ as a substitutionary sacrifice, and it accepts his imputed righteousness. Saving faith is not just a shallow intellectual confession of impersonal facts; it is a deep and genuine commitment to center one's hope in Christ. The preeminent term by which salvation is received (in the biblical record) is "faith" or "belief." Our "faithfulness," "obedience," or "works" are not the issue in justification before God through the Gospel. "Repentance" leading to salvation should be understood as a changing of mind concerning Jesus as the Christ. The notion of having to successfully turn from every known sin in order to be saved is not warranted. Justification (declared righteous by faith) and sanctification (the progressive transformation to righteous behavior) should not be mixed even though the latter flows out of the former. It is possible for a genuine Christian to be "carnal" or live as though he or she was not a Christian. But this state is unnatural, and in most cases temporary. To insist on complete submission to God's will in every area of life (before one can call themselves a Christian) is contrary to biblical testimony and human experience. Easy-believism and a front-end-loading of the gospel are both threats to the orthodox faith.

12. How should I apply the Ten Commandments to my life as a believer?

The Ten Commandments are very helpful for the Christian's understanding of God's kingdom and His expectations of those who live in it. These moral standards are consistent and progressively revealed as a mirror of God's nature.

   a.   Kingdom ethics are revealed subtly in creation—human conscience and nature, Gen.26:5, Rom.1:18–19,32, 23:14–15

   b.   Kingdom ethics are revealed superficially in the Ten Commandments—Law of Moses

   c.   Kingdom ethics are revealed supremely in the person of Christ—The Holy Spirit, Gal.6:2

The Law of Moses reflects an eternal ethic and as such is applicable to the present church as an ethical guide. As a covenant of works (with blessings and cursing dependent upon faithfulness to the law of Moses), it is terminated in Christ and not applicable to the present church age.

13. What do we mean by Christian freedom?

The challenge is not to win freedom but to walk in it. The freedom is already ours in Christ. We must claim it by faith. If we don't use what is available to us, we are little better than if we didn't have it. Experiencing freedom from condemnation is a key to experiencing freedom from sin. We can't obtain freedom from the condemnation of the law by conquering the power of the flesh. It is by dying with Christ that we are free. This means that the freedom is not experiential sinlessness so much as claiming and resting in Christ's holiness, which is imputed to us.

Professional therapists observe that unless a person senses they are loved just as they are, they will not change to what they should be. The path to freedom is death (through union with Christ's death as pictured in water baptism). It is not the law but the cross, and not the flesh but the Spirit, which is the path to freedom. Freedom from sinful compulsions starts with death as a living sacrifice.

Christian freedom takes two forms

Freedom from Condemnation of the Law	*Freedom from Control by the Flesh*
Legal effect – no condemnation	*Legal effect –* no need to sin
Experiential effect – no feeling of alienation	*Experiential effect –* no compulsion to sin
Romans 8:1–3, Ephesians 2:8–9, Galatians 5:1–4	*Romans 8:4, Ephesians 2:10, Galatians 5:13–17*

14. How do I know I am experiencing the right kind of freedom from the law?

Signs of bondage to the law

When I am in bondage I have a moral want-to that seems blocked by a moral power failure that leaves me in shame and toxic guilt. Paul expresses this lack of freedom in Romans 7:24, "*wretched man that I am, the very thing I don't want to do, I do.*" I have little interest in understanding or awareness of altering my self-protective strategies. Obedience is experienced as a painful burden. Fear and anger are characteristics of my life. I see life's circumstances as threatening and burdensome. I live in fear of condemnation unless I can "get it together" so as to obey.

Characteristics of the person who is free from the law

A person who is free from the law experiences little or no sense of this fear of condemnation even though their obedience is less than perfect or complete. Obedience to the

Spirit, a natural impulse for the believer, may not always be followed, but is now released in the life of the believer. Love of God and others is no longer a dutiful burden. The fruit of the Spirit is released in and through the believer. There is a deep sense of peace in life on the basis of faith in Christ's work *for* not *through* the believer. Opportunities to respond to circumstances with Godly attitudes and actions are welcomed without fear of failure to be perfect.

15. Should the Christian expect to live a life free from all known sin?

The normal Christian life involves an intense inner spiritual struggle. Galatians 5:17 "*For the flesh sets its desire against the Spirit, and the Spirit against the flesh; for these are in opposition to one another, so that you may not do the things that you please.*" If your Christian experience is an easy one, then I am saying you are out of touch with the circumstances of life. While we are in this body of flesh, we will not be able to do everything we would like to do. I find those who claim to experience consistent and complete victory over sin in their lives do one of a number of things.

They make that claim based upon a FAITH–confession, not experience. "I'm claiming it by faith." They also tend to define sin in a superficial way. They limit coveting to *obsessive* lusting through fleshly appetites. I call this "law-lite" in that it disregards the "little sins" like envy, coveting, anger, pride, etc. as though they don't really count. They define victory in a superficial way. They also tend to define victory as the absence of any *willing* violation of the laws of God—no premeditated sin. They may even lie about their moral conduct. When someone claims to "have total victory over sin," I conclude they have disqualified themselves by the sin of lying.

There is an impulse in every fallen human to resist the things of God. We can identify with Paul in Romans 7:21–24, "*I find then the principle that evil is present in me, the one who wishes to do good. For I joyfully concur with the law of God in the inner man, but I see a different law in the members of my body, waging war against the law of my mind, and making me a prisoner of the law or sin which is in my members. Wretched man that I am! Who will set me free from the body of this death?"* While in this body of death, the impulse to sin will be with us.

"The flesh" in Paul's writing has many meanings: *"a thorn in the flesh"* (2 Cor.12:7) means the material body. *"Jesus is the son of David according to the flesh"* (Rom.1:3) refers to Jesus' human ancestry. *"Wise after the flesh"* (1 Cor.1:16) refers to human nature apart from the indwelling Spirit of Christ. In Galatians 5:17 Paul uses the word to describe an impulse—the driving passion of a fallen human race that is worldly as opposed to godly, rebellious as opposed to obedient, and carnal as opposed to spiritual. The flesh refers to the old self in Adam as opposed to the new self in Christ. The flesh is often provoked by the world and is exposed by the law. It leads to death. It wants *autonomy*—to do what is right in one's own eye. It wants *relativity*—no absolute commitments. It wants *contingency*—life to follow predictable cause and effect rules. It wants *temporality*—benefits in this life and soon. After four years of seminary and over forty years of ministry, my flesh has not improved one bit. It is incapable of being reformed.

In Galatians 5:17 Paul tells us there is also a supernatural impulse given to every Christian to follow God. It is the Spirit. "The Spirit" is used to describe: the spirit world over the physical, the spirit of mankind, and the Spirit of God or of Christ. This impulse to follow God comes from the Spirit of Christ, which is given to the believer at the time he or she trusts his or her life to Christ. It is an ability to understand the ways of God. It is a desire to walk in his ways. It is a source of energy to actually obey those ways. It is a source of hope that enables Christians to sacrifice self as they wait for the promises of God's kingdom. A great dissonance exists in the Christian between the flesh and the Spirit that will not be resolved until we are free from this earthly body of death.

16. How can I have victory over sin in my life?

There are three popular plans to achieve victory over sin.

Plan #1 Face the demands of the law in the power of my flesh—discipline, will power, conditioning, etc.
Plan #2 Face the demands of the law in the power of the Spirit—prayer, faith, promises of God, etc.
Plan #3 Set the mind on Christ and union with Him under the New Covenant of grace, not on the law or personal performance. It is this third plan that is emphasized in this book. Use the law as a guide to our calling, not as a measure of our worth. Fix our hope for perfection on Christ's return and accept the process of growth in this life. Get our eyes off self and onto Christ.

17. Is uniform sustained avoidance of all personal sin possible in this life?

In theory it is possible to live a life without sin, but in practice it does not happen. The following questions need to be answered before we can claim to have full victory over sin in our experience.

Can Matthew 22:37–39 be satisfied? "*And He said to him, 'You shall love the Lord your God with all your heart, and with all your soul, and with all your mind. This is the great and foremost commandment. And a second is like it, you shall love your neighbor as yourself.*" If I limit the issue to "known sin," don't I give a pass to all sociopaths? 1 Corinthians 4:4, "*I am conscious of nothing against myself, yet I am not by this acquitted; but the one who examines me is the Lord.*" How can we discern our own motives when our hearts are deceitful? Is it ever possible to know we are not sinning? Does Scripture recognize two distinct classes of believers—victorious and defeated?

18. How should we view water baptism?

What the "altar call" was to early American revivalists, water baptism was to the first century church. It was the way a believer expressed his or her entrance into the faith. People came to the altar to express faith, not to get it; so it was with baptism as well.

As I have already indicated in this book, baptism can be compared to a marriage ceremony. The marriage ceremony is not the place where two people really decided to commit their lives to each other, nor is it the place where they consummated their union. Water baptism is not the point where saving faith comes but rather the public and official celebration / initiation of the person into the visible church (body of believers). It is understandable that water baptism would be spoken of (in Scripture and culture) as the point of initiation (like the marriage ceremony).

Another analogy might be circumcision (Col.2:11–12). In this case water baptism, like circumcision, is an outward sign of one's identification with the covenant community. Under the Old Covenant it was a national community identified by circumcision. Under the New Covenant it is a spiritual community of faith identified by water baptism.

Another analogy can be made with our Lord's reference to the bread and cup—"This is my body / blood." The bread and cup were not physically His body and blood (Jesus was physically holding the elements), yet it was not an inappropriate use of language to refer to these symbols as such. In the same way it is not strange for the biblical writers to refer to *"baptism"* and *"washing away of sins"* when describing the justification of faith. In saying this I am maintaining a distinction between saving faith (justification, regeneration by the Holy Spirit) and water baptism (the official expression of faith). It is the inner faith not the outer expression that unites a person with Christ. This was the gist of Jesus' conflict with the Pharisees who insisted that nothing really counted before God until the outer demands of the law were satisfied. The outer expression of faith is nonetheless very important because it identifies a person outwardly with the church.

Appendix #2
Discipleship Salvation

A Parable Analogy

The following parable of grace lays out the issue clearly distinguishing Discipleship Salvation from Free Grace.

A wealthy man had three sons who were bound for college but each son had no money to enter the elite school they had chosen to attend. To the first son the father said, "I will give you a job to earn money so you can one day pay for your education." To the second son he said, "I will loan you enough money to go to college, but if you fail to make good grades or drop out, you will be expected to pay me back all I have loaned you." To the third son he said, "I will give you enough money to go to college with the expectation you will finish with good grades—but even if you do not meet my expectations, the money is a free gift to you." Now which of the three sons' experience illustrates the grace of the father? The answer is that each of the stories illustrates the father's grace but in different ways and to different extents.

Which of these three sons' experiences best illustrates the Christian Gospel? The first son's experience is not unlike the posture of the legalist whereby God enabled the believer (by grace) to earn his way to eternal life. We might say in this case the Gospel is "front end loaded" with the requirement of faithfulness or obedience. The second son's experience can be likened to those who "back end load" the Gospel with obedience. The grace of God in this case is conditioned upon the faithfulness of the person after he receives salvation. If the believer fails to be faithful, he loses his eternal life. The third son's experience can be likened to radical grace where the gift is unconditional. It is expected that the believer will be faithful and meet the demands of the Kingdom, but even if he does not, he still retains the gift of eternal life. There is general agreement among Protestants that the experience of the first son (the

Roman Catholic position) does not represent the Gospel. But there is not a clear agreement as to which of the other two sons best illustrates the true Gospel. Is the gift of eternal life conditioned on the moral conduct (regeneration) of the recipient? Is true faith marked by obedience?

At stake is the nature of saving faith? How is the Christian community to view a person who professes to believe in Christ as their Savior from the penalty of sin and yet lives a life that is outwardly unchanged and worldly? If a person's life shows no clear evidence of following Christ after professing to be a Christian, should the Christian community recognize them as true believers; or should they be viewed as false believers who have deceived themselves? When the gospel is presented and people are encouraged to trust Christ, what kind of repentance is necessary? Must they repent of all sinful deeds, or is it just repentance from false beliefs about Christ as one's redeemer that is necessary?

Justification and Regeneration

The Protestant Reformation highlighted many points of tension within Christian theology not the least of which was the relationship between "justification" (being declared righteous by and before God) and "regeneration" (the beginning of the process of being made righteous by the renewal of the inner human nature). While both justification and regeneration are a necessary and actual part of saving faith, there is some controversy as to their relationship. The reformers (Luther and Calvin) distinguished the two. They viewed "justification" as forensic, external to human behavior, the imputation of Christ's righteousness to the believer. Luther, in reference to "justification", spoke of the "alien righteousness of Christ" or the "passive righteousness" of the believer. Regeneration, on the other hand, was viewed by the reformers as the indwelling of Christ's life in the believer. This was the new birth of a new nature that started a process of spiritual renewal resulting in "sanctification" or practiced righteousness. We might say that salvation by faith included 1) being placed "in Christ" (positionally) as well as 2) being born again of the Spirit so as to have "Christ in us."

The Two Spheres of Repentance

Justification	*Regeneration*
Being declared righteous by God and before God	Becoming righteous from the inside out
Being "in Christ"	Having Christ "in us"
Imputed righteousness of Christ	Imparted righteousness of the Holy Spirit
Legal position	Experiential posture
Perfect and complete on the basis of faith alone	The beginning of the process of sanctification

The Roman Catholic position combines "regeneration" as a necessary and key part of "justification." Protestants have traditionally made a hard and clear distinction between the two. In some ways the discipleship / salvation controversy is a revisiting of this issue from within the protestant camp.

A Self-Test

Let's try to find out where you are on this issue? What is your understanding of saving faith? Which of the following statements BEST captures your understanding? The following statements represent the breadth of perspectives among professing evangelical Christians. The issue has to do with the relationship between faith and faithfulness.

1. While all who will be saved are saved on the basis of Christ's substitutionary atonement, it is possible that some will be saved without hearing the gospel story.

2. In order to be saved you must simply hear the gospel and pray the sinner's prayer.

3. In order to be saved you must simply profess sincere faith in Christ as God.

4. In order to be saved you must change your mind with regard to Christ and place your faith in Him as your righteousness apart from yourself.

5. In order to be saved you must place your trust in Christ and turn away from all known sin in your life (at the time of your profession of faith).

6. In order to be saved you must continually place every area of your life under the Lordship (control) of Christ.

7. In order to be saved you must place your faith in Christ and continue to abstain from all known sin with the power of the Holy Spirit.

8. In order to be saved you must place your faith in Christ as Lord of every area of your life and be baptized by immersion for the remission of sins.

The Discipleship Salvation (DS) Position

There are four basic beliefs associated with those who argue for the "Discipleship Salvation" (DS) perspective.

1. Not everyone who professes to be a Christian really has saving faith.

2. We will know true Christian faith by seeing obedience to the law of God in the lives of those who have it.

3. We must come to Christ and follow after Him if He is to justify us.

4. A true believer cannot continue to live in sin.

Those who advocate the DS position believe they are protecting the true gospel from the unbiblical notion of antinomianism (lawlessness). They hold the following beliefs:

1. A person cannot receive the benefits of salvation by just intellectually confessing Jesus as Savior.

2. There must be repentance from all known sinful deeds if a person is to be truly justified.

3. Saving faith results in the acknowledgment of Jesus as Lord and is identified by a posture of active obedience and conformity to the moral teaching of Jesus.

4. Justification is by faith apart from works, but the required marker of justification is a changed life. If the life is not changed, the faith is not a justifying faith.

5. The fear of radical grace is that it will undermine the fear of a holy God. It is believed that "Where (radical) grace abounds, sin will all the more abound."

Jesus indicated there is a high cost for discipleship (Matt.10:38; 16:24; Lk.14:25–27), and true commitment demands complete surrender of everything (Matt.19:16, 21; Mk.10:23; Lk.14:33). Several of the calls to salvation in Acts use the word repentance (Acts 2:38; 11:18), which is always defined as "turning from sin." John the Baptist and Christ in the early part of their ministry say the same thing (Mk.1:4; Matt.3:2; 11:20). These passages are seen as proof that one must fully repent (from all sin) and make a total commitment to Christ before one can be saved. It is the will of God for all men to be preserved meaning all men will continue in a godly life until the end (1 Tim.4:16; Heb.10:36). If anyone does not persevere, he must doubt whether his faith is true and therefore if his salvation is secure.

Several "tests" have been proposed to determine if a professing believer is truly saved such as John 8:31 where we read, "*Jesus therefore was saying to those Jews who had believed Him, 'If you abide in My word then you are truly disciples of Mine;'*" later in verse 44 He says, "*you are of your father the devil*" suggesting they really did not believe unto salvation. See also John 2:23–24.

Much of the support for DS comes from the teaching of Jesus in the Synoptic Gospels where there are many demands or conditions that are linked to forgiveness and eternal life. Matthew offers some examples.

1. As some Jewish religious leaders came to John the Baptist for baptism they were turned away with these words *"bring forth fruit in keeping with your repentance"* (Matt.2:8).

2. Jesus began his ministry with words like *"unless your righteousness surpasses that of the scribes and Pharisees, you shall not enter the kingdom of heaven."* (Matt.5:20).

3. The Sermon on the Mount is full of warnings about failing to fulfill the spirit of the law. *"Whoever shall say 'you fool' shall be guilty enough to go into the hell of fire."* (Matt.5:22–23). Matthew 5:29–30 *"And if your right eye makes you stumble, tear it our, and throw it from you; for it is better for you that one of the parts of your body perish, than for your whole body to be thrown into hell. And if your right hand makes you stumble, cut it off, and throw it from you for it is better for you that one of the parts of your body perish, than for your whole body to be into hell."* (also Matt.18:8– 9). Matthew 6:14–15 *"For if you forgive men for their transgressions, your heavenly Father will also forgive you. But if you do not forgive men, then your Father will not forgive your transgressions."* Matthew 7:19 *"Every tree that does not bear good fruit is cut down and thrown into the fire."* Matthew 7:21–23 *"Not everyone who says to Me, 'Lord, Lord,' will enter the kingdom of heaven; but he who does the will of My Father who is in heaven. Many will say to Me on that day, 'Lord, Lord, did we not prophesy in Your name, and in Your name cast out demons, and in Your name perform many miracles?' And then I will declare to them, 'I never knew you; depart form Me, you who practice lawlessness.'"* Matthew 10:33 *"But whoever shall deny Me before men, I will also deny him before My Father who is in heaven."*

4. Jesus seems clear in indicating that the unrighteous will not be a part of his spiritual family and will be judged harshly. Matthew12:36–37 *"And I say to you,*

that every careless word that men shall speak, they shall render account for it in the day of judgment. For by your words you shall be justified, and by your words you shall be condemned." Matthew 12:50 *"for whoever shall do the will of My Father who is in heaven, he is My brother and sister and mother."* Matthew 13:49–50 *"So it will be at the end of he age; the angels shall come forth, and take out the wicked from among the righteous, and will cast them into the furnace of fire; there shall be weeping and gnashing of teeth."* In Matthew 18:21–35 Jesus tells us a story about an ungrateful servant who is forgiven much but refuses to forgive a small debt. In the story the master repents of his forgiving the ungrateful steward and forces him to pay. Jesus then concludes with, *"So shall My heavenly Father also do to you, if each of you does not forgive his brother from your heart."*

5.   In Matthew 19:16–26 Jesus confronts the Rich Young Ruler who asks what he must do to obtain eternal life. Jesus responds with, *"If you wish to be complete, go and sell your possessions and give to the poor, and you shall have treasure in heaven; and come, follow Me."*

6.   In Matthew 24:42–51 Jesus tells the story of the slave who wrongly assumes his master will not come to checkup on him so he behaves badly. Jesus concludes the story with, *"the master of that slave will come on a day when he does not expect him and at an hour which he does not know. And shall cut him in pieces and assign him a place with the hypocrites; weeping shall be there and the gnashing of teeth."*

7.   In Matthew 25:14–30 Jesus gives us the parable of the talents and says of the servant who did not wisely invest his talents, *"And cast out the worthless slave into the outer darkness; in that place there shall be weeping and gnashing of teeth."* Jesus' teaching on the final judgment of the nations concludes with these words, *"Then He will answer them, saying, 'truly I say to you,*

to the extent that you did not do it to one of the least of these, you did not do it to Me.' And they will go away into eternal punishment, but the righteous into eternal life." (Matt.25:45–46). It is hard to see how many of these texts can be harmonized with the Gospel of Grace in the Epistles. Could it be that Jesus' teaching is set in a unique and different context than that of Paul? This relationship between Jesus' teaching (in Matthew, Mark, and Luke) and that of Paul in his Epistles is a part of the debate.

Terms used to describe opponents of DS include the following:

1. Antinomian—opposed to any moral law

2. Easy-believism—no moral demands are made on those who are saved

3. Cheap grace—grace demanding nothing from those who receive it but intellectual assent to a doctrine

The Free Grace (FG) position

Those who advocate a "Free Grace" (FG) position claim they are protecting the gospel of grace from the unbiblical heresy of salvation by works. They hold the following beliefs:

1. The wedding of faith and faithfulness (obedience) is contrary to the gospel of grace.

2. While it is normally expected that justification by faith will result in sanctification (faithfulness) in practice, it is not always the case at least in an outward sense.

3. Often people come to surrender control of their lives to the power of Christ sometime after they have experienced His gracious acceptance through faith.

4. Once we begin to require conformity to holiness as a part of saving faith, we have the difficult task of determining which sins a believer can continue to struggle with or continue in and still be received as a Christian.

5. Is the church consistent? Some churches will permit a true Christian to have unresolved anger, jealousy, covetousness, gluttony, materialism, etc. when they will not tolerate substance abuse, fornication, lying, etc.?

    Advocates of FG point out that the gospel of the kingdom (focused on obedience) proclaimed by Jesus in Mathew, Mark, and Luke was distinct in some ways from the gospel of the cross and resurrection preached by Paul. They point to a number of passages that clearly speak of faith (with no mention of faithfulness) as the means by which salvation is given.

*   ***Acts 11:17*** *"If God therefore gave to them the same gift as He gave to us also after believing in the Lord Jesus Christ, who was I that I could stand in God's way?" (to baptize)*

*   ***John 1:12*** *"But as many as received Him, to them He gave the right to become children of God, even to those who believe in His name:"*

*   ***John 3:14–16*** *"that whoever believes may in Him have eternal life."*

*   ***John 7:37–40*** *"every one who beholds the Son, and believes in Him, may have eternal life;"*

*   ***Acts 10:43*** *"that through His name every one who believes in Him has received forgiveness of sins."*

*   ***Acts 13:38–39*** *"through Him everyone who believes is freed"*

*   ***Acts 15:9*** *"cleansing their hearts by faith."*

*   ***Romans 3:21–4:8*** *"But to the one who does not work, but believes in Him who justifies the ungodly, his faith is reckoned as righteousness."*

*   ***Romans 9:33*** *"and he who believes in Him shall not be disappointed."*

- **Romans 10:10** *"for with the heart man believes, resulting in righteousness, and with the mouth he confesses resulting in salvation."*

- **1 Corinthians.1:21** *"to save those who believe"*

- **Galatians 2:16** *"a man is not justified by the works of the law but through faith in Christ Jesus"*

- **Galatians 3:2** *"Did you receive the Spirit by the works of the law, or by hearing with faith?"*

- **Galatians 3:26** *"For you are all sons of God through faith in Christ Jesus."*

- **Ephesians 1:13** *"having also believed, you were sealed in Him"*

- **Ephesians 2:8–10** *"For by grace you have been saved through faith; and that not of yourselves, it is the gift of God"*

- **1 Timothy 1:16** *"for those who would believe in Him for eternal life."*

- **1 Peter 1:8–9** *"and though you have not seen Him, you love Him, and though you do not see Him now, but believe in Him, you greatly rejoice with joy inexpressible and full of glory, obtaining as the outcome of your faith the salvation of your souls."*

- **1 John 5:1** *"Whoever believes that Jesus is the Christ is born of God"*

- **1 John 5:13** *"These things I have written to you who believe in the name of the Son of God, in order that you may know that you have eternal life."*

Advocates of FG point to biblical distinctions between justification, sanctification, and glorification that are not properly established in DS theology. In the Scripture salvation is almost exclusively seen as eternal life in heaven and rarely, if ever, seen as present sanctification. This creates a problem in interpreting passages such as Philippians 2:12 *"work out your salvation with fear."* Although Christ makes distinctions between the free offer of salvation to all men (Lk.14:15–24) and the high cost of discipleship (Lk.14:25–27) resulting in reward, this distinction is ignored in Discipleship theology.

Repentance in Greek (*metenoesan)* means literally "to change one's mind." It is understood in DS circles to include "turning from all sin." The Greek translation of the Old Testament used *metenoesan* for God (Ex.34:2; Jer.26:13) who was obviously not turning from sin. It is true that John the Baptist and Christ did urge the Jews to repent from sin (Jn.1:23; Matt.4:17) to usher in the kingdom and covenant Christ was to fulfill. But note that this repentance from sin was not for justification. It rather identified individuals with the imminent Kingdom of God. For salvation repentance should be understood as a change of mind about who Christ is. Peter explained to the Jews who Christ was and then asks them to change their minds about rejecting Him and receive salvation (Acts 2:36-38).

Although many DS proponents teach eternal security (that salvation cannot be lost once it is received), they teach that assurance of salvation can only come when a believer is persevering in good works. It must logically follow that every time a believer struggles in sin or doubt, they are forced to question whether or not they are saved (elect). The peace God promises and the fact one can know for certain he or she is saved (1 Jn.5:13) is problematic in DS teaching. Believers need to base their assurance on the objective truth about what the Word says regarding someone who has placed his or her faith in Christ's provision (Acts 10:43) rather than in the subjective truth of how well they conform to the holy nature of God.

The New Testament makes it very clear there is a possibility a true believer may not continue in good works and may face severe discipline (Heb.10:26–27) even unto death (1 Cor.5:5; Jas.5:20–21). If it is true that all will persevere, these passages make little sense. What are we to make of the repeated calls for obedience by the Apostles addressed to the churches in the Epistles? If indeed Christians do not continue in sin, why did they have to encourage them to shape up and stop? Why were believers repeatedly exhorted to forbear with one another and forgive one another? There are several examples of confirmed believers that did not live as faithful disciples. The primitive church in Corinth is one example. Paul exhorts sinning Christians to repent and obey not in order to prove or maintain saving faith but rather because they are called and equipped to follow Christ in response to God's grace (Rom.12:1–2).

When we look at the passages that lay down the requirements for being a disciple (a true Christian by DS views), we find a number of requirements that no one fully meets. The consistent DS view must insist these demands be met fully before a person can be saved.

- "Deny himself"– make no provision for self. (Matt.16:24)

- "Take up his cross" – share the suffering of Christ. (Matt.16:24–27)

- "Follow Me"– not double minded. (Matt.16:24–27)

- "Loses his life" – make no provision for this present temporal life. (Matt.16:24–27)

- "Whoever is ashamed of Me" – bold unapologetic witness. (Lk.9:26)

- "Hate your family" (Matt.10:37, Lk.14:26) – put Christ above one's natural family.

- "Forsake all" (Lk.14:33) – hold on to nothing in this world.

- "Abide in His Word" (Jn.8:30–31) – continued unfailing obedience to the Scripture.

- "Him who overcomes" (Rev.2:7) – brings moral life under successful management.

  How many of us qualify by these standards? We may be committed to them but that is not enough. We must obey them fully or we cannot be Jesus' disciple or a part of his kingdom, the community of the saved.

Summary of Distinctives

Four different understandings of the relationship between faith and moral obedience are compared in this chart.

The Jewish position	*The Roman Catholic position*	*Discipleship Salvation position*	*The Free Grace position*
Obedience is all that matters	Obedience is necessary for faith	Obedience is a marker of faith	Obedience is a fruit of faith
Obedience = Faith	Faith = Obedience	Faith / Obedience	Faith > Obedience

1. The Roman Catholic position could be viewed as (Faith + works = salvation). Works are the form of saving faith.

2. The Calvinistic and Arminian positions could be characterized as (Faith = salvation + works). Works are the sign or marker of faith.

3. The radical (free) grace position could be understood as (Faith = salvation which sets the stage for works but is authentic and effective without works). Works are the fruit of faith not the essence of it.

4. True faith is a deep personal commitment. It is more than intellectual awareness or assent.

5. True faith may be authentic even if it does not take the form of faithfulness although it normally leads to faithfulness.

6. True faith always produces inner fruit (a changed heart).

7. True faith normally produces outer fruit (faithfulness).

Saint Augustine wisely recognized various degrees of knowledge and commitment. The following chart illustrates five levels of commitment. Note the distinction between Level #3 and #4. Does true saving faith require a level #4 or #5 commitment (The Discipleship Salvation view), or is level #3 all that is required (Free Grace view)?

> **Level #1**
>
> **Intellectual awareness**
> **"knowing about Christ"**

Free Grace people are
sometimes accused of
believing this is all that is
necessary for salvation.

> **Level #2**
>
> **Intellectual assent**
> **"superficial faith confession"**
> **Jas.2:19**

This is what Free Grace
people believe is necessary
for salvation.

> **Level #3**
>
> **Heartfelt Trust**
> **"heartfelt confession**
> **of faith in Christ"**
> **Rom.10:9**

This is what some Discipleship Salvation people believe
is necessary for salvation.

> **Level #4**
>
> **Commitment to holy living**
> **(a pure heart)**

This is what other Discipleship Salvation people believe
is necessary for salvation.

> **Level #5**
>
> **Obedience (a pure life)**

What is Important?

Some basic issues need to be protected in this debate.

1. Salvation is by grace through faith apart from human
    merit. It is possible to have true saving faith and yet go
    to one's grave with unresolved moral conflicts in life.

2. True faith is a deep commitment of one's life. It is not a
    superficial confession of words.

3. It is possible to have true saving faith and look
    (outwardly at times) like a non–Christian. This was the
    case in first century Corinth.

4. True saving faith always bears fruit – at least inwardly (new birth) and often outwardly (changed conduct).

5. Repentance from sin is always needed as a part of our approach to God in worship. This implies that there will always be unresolved sins in a person's life. The Pharisee was criticized because he felt he no longer had sins to confess.

Good intentions are sometimes cited as sufficient, but this is without Biblical support. No one is perfect, but it is believed we can have perfect intentions. If it is true that "we are not saved by our good works," it must also be true that we are not saved by our good intentions. The Jewish leaders of Paul's day had good intentions, but this did not save them. What saves us is not our works or our intentions but the work of Christ and our transfer of trust in anything and everything else to Him.

Marriage can serve as an example of our relationship with God. When a man and a woman go to the altar and make a marriage covenant vow, it is expected they will live as husband and wife. It would be technically possible for them to be truly married and not live as though they were married, but this would be most unusual. On the other hand, it is quite possible they would not live out their marriage vows perfectly. There would be times when they would act selfishly and perhaps even unfaithfully, but they would still be married. So it is in our relationship with Christ. At baptism we enter into a covenant relationship with Christ. It is expected we will also follow Him as disciples, but we will not do so perfectly. There may be times when we are quite rebellious to the point of acting as though we were not following Him at all. We might still, however, be true believers. The Free Grace position maintains that we are secure "in Christ" by faith in his righteousness not ours.

Summary Conclusion

1. If one calls on Christ to save him from the penalty of sin, one is confessing and submitting to Christ as Master or Lord of one very important area of life—the soul's need for a substitutionary sacrifice and an imputed righteousness before a holy God.

2. Saving faith is not just a shallow intellectual confession of impersonal facts; it is a deep, genuine commitment to center one's hope in Christ for justification before God.

3. It is possible for a person to make a false profession of faith and actually believe he or she is a Christian when in fact they are not.

4. The preeminent term by which salvation is received (in the Scripture) is "faith" or "belief." Our "faithfulness", "obedience" or "works" are not the issue in the grace that justifies the believer before God.

5. "Repentance" unto salvation is understood as turning from one's self-sufficiency (rather than every known sin) to a commitment that Jesus is the Redeemer Christ.

6. Saving faith is linked to both justification (being declared perfectly righteous) and regeneration (leading to sanctification by the indwelling Spirit of Christ).

7. Justification (declared righteous by faith) and sanctification (progressively demonstrating righteous behavior) should not be equated or confused even though the latter flows out of the former.

8. Repentance that leads to eternal life is distinct from "good works" but is the basis of and for the purpose of "good works."

9. It is possible for a genuine Christian to be "carnal" or live as though he or she was not a Christian. But this state is unnatural and normally is temporary.

10. To insist on complete submission to God's will in every area of life (before one can call themselves a Christian) is contrary to Biblical testimony and human experience.

Appendix #3
Church Discipline

Sometimes it is necessary for the Christian community to be the instrument of discipline. Paul speaks of this in 2 Corinthians 7:8–10: *"For though I caused you sorrow by my letter, I do not regret it; though I did regret it—{for} I see that that letter caused you sorrow, though only for a while—I now rejoice, not that you were made sorrowful, but that you were made sorrowful to {the point of} repentance; for you were made sorrowful according to {the will of} God, in order that you might not suffer loss in anything through us. For the sorrow that is according to {the will of} God produces a repentance without regret, {leading} to salvation; but the sorrow of the world produces death."*

In this passage Paul prescribed discipline and recognized the pain it caused. But he also understands the fruit it brings, *"in order that you might not suffer loss."* Paul did not want the Corinthians to miss out on the joy, fruitfulness, and peace of God's kingdom as expressed in the church. Some have understood this passage to refer to the eternal state of the sinner in question (vs. 11–12), but it is also very likely that Paul has more than eternity in mind. He does not want them to lose out on "anything." The specific sin in question is not as important as the function of discipline in response to it. When we act in sinful, selfish, destructive ways, we exclude ourselves from many of God's blessings and from peace for our souls.

It is unfortunate that so few churches exercise loving discipline or know how to practice it in ways that actually work to produce repentance and restoration. The following observations come from personal experience having been on both sides of the table with respect to church discipline.

First, a congregation's leadership should be prepared to handle discipline situations before they occur. This will enable a level of objectivity that may not be possible once real personalities are involved. This ordinarily is the task of elders or recognized leaders in the church. Thinking through the "what if" situations is an important part of good leadership.

Second, it is important to answer the question, what behaviors or attitudes require discipline? I would hope mature leaders would look beneath some of the typical overt transgressions (unorthodox doctrine, open immorality, blasphemy [gross disrespect for Christ], divisiveness, and so on) to the heart attitude of the person. Discipline is seldom effective if it only addresses the superficial actions and not the heart. This is not to suggest that overt behavior is not an issue. I suggest however that overt behavior is seldom the whole issue or the root issue.

Third, close relationships within a Christian community are vital to constructive church discipline. We will have a hard time correcting someone who senses we do not know or love them. One of the reasons church discipline fails is due to a lack of understanding and love on the part of those doing the correcting. Before steps are taken, there should be lots of talking and listening to promote understanding.

Fourth, the pattern of Matthew 18 is full of practical and wise advice: *"15 And if your brother sins, go and reprove him in private; if he listens to you, you have won your brother. 16 But if he does not listen to you, take one or two more with you, so that by the mouth of two or three witnesses every fact may be confirmed. 17 And if he refuses to listen to them, tell it to the church; and if he refuses to listen even to the church, let him be to you as a Gentile and a tax-gatherer."* This passage first indicates that confrontation should only be made public as a last resort. Public correction and discipline may leave a person open to a lot of unfair and uncontrolled attacks. Public exposure also invites divisiveness in the community. Inevitably there will be people who see things differently and take a stand for or against the leaders or the person being disciplined. So as a rule try to avoid public exposure. The second bit of wisdom from this passage underscores the importance of not acting alone in confronting someone who is resistant. The third bit of wisdom is to not rush the process of confrontation. Respect the person by increasing the pressure slowly and with the support of others. The goal here is to try to understand where the root problem lies. Many people will respond positively when they sense others are trying to help them manage the challenges of life in ways that are consistent with their faith and not destructive to their relationships with God and others.

Fifth, deal with present problems not past problems. Discipline is not punishment for past sins, immaturity, or ignorance; it is correction for present rebellious attitudes. Once a person has repented, they do not need discipline; they need support, encouragement, and affirmation. It is interesting that the father of the prodigal son was quick to throw a party once he came home. Too often discipline is applied long after repentance has taken place as a form of punishment for the hurt that has been caused by the offender. And we might add that seldom is a party thrown for the penitent sinners in our churches. One of the most powerful tools in the healing of the wayward son in this story is the lavish and unexpected party thrown by the very person he most offended. It is the radical display of love and forgiveness from the Father that most effectively medicates the shame of the son.

Sixth, an advocate or spokesperson should be assigned to the person being disciplined. This should be a person trusted by both the leadership and the one under discipline. The role of the advocate is first to advise the person under discipline in how to cooperate and respond. It will be hard for the person being disciplined to be objective in the discipline process, and a trusted coach can be critical to a good outcome. The advocate also should speak on behalf of the person being disciplined and defend their rights in the process. Things will be said and done that are well meaning but may seem unfair. If those being disciplined are left to defend themselves, their words will almost always be used against them later. It is generally best for a spokesperson to do most of the talking. When a person being disciplined offers explanations, they are often heard as excuses. The advocate's role should extend to the whole process even after discipline is carried out so the disciplined person does not feel abandoned and so the leadership knows how the person is responding.

Finally, the Christian community must be eager to restore penitent sinners not just discard them or disengage with them once they repent. A healthy church should look at discipline as a showcase for the practice of grace and the gospel. Confronting spiritual rebellion and comforting those who repent are both vital roles for a healthy church. In so doing, the church becomes a light to the world with the Christian gospel.

Discipline through the church is necessary when discipline from God's hand through natural circumstances is not forthcoming. The goal is not punishment for sin, nor is it justice, but rather grace and salvation. The purpose is to keep a person not only from abusing others and themselves, but also to assure they not miss out on the fullness of God's blessing. This is peacemaking in action.

A point to ponder

Loving discipline must end once repentance is complete lest it become a destructive hindrance to grace.

How Should a Person Respond to Church Discipline?

If you are undergoing discipline, first cooperate with the process and trust that God is going to use this in your life for the better even though it may seem unjust at the time. Any lack of cooperation will certainly make the process longer, more painful, and more easily corrupted by injustice. Satan loves a good fight between Christians and this is an easy setting for one. The best indication of the true condition of your heart will be your response to discipline especially when you feel it is unjust.

Second, don't use the "illegal procedure" card. There is a strong tendency to counterattack by claiming that the corrective discipline is not being handled properly or according to Scripture. No doubt there will be things that could be done better, but when you try to derail the process or throw it out of court; you are only hurting yourself. This is the time to be quick to hear and slow to speak and slow to anger. It is not your place to monitor or critique the process.

Third, anything you say will probably be misunderstood and used against you, so keep your comments short and be careful when you vent your feelings. If you make an apology to an offended person or group, make it short, sincere, and specific. Any excuses, explanations, or shifting of blame will tend to nullify the apology and simply mean you will have to do it over again later. You don't want to do this more than once, so do it right the first time.

Fourth, work hard at the process of repentance. This means striving for insight—"getting it." It means making hard decisions of change in attitude and conduct. It may mean offering and making restitution where necessary. It means not demanding restoration especially before full repentance has taken place. True repentance often is a process requiring patience and time. Keep at it until those in authority over you are convinced that things have changed in your soul. A common problem with people who have been disciplined is their tendency to declare the process over before it really is. While we may be able to repent of certain behaviors speedily, it is unlikely that the underlying attitudes can be quickly recognized or changed.

Many people who are disciplined by a church do not respond very well. This may be because of the way the discipline is administered, but more often it is the result of a hard heart and stubborn spirit of rebellion in the person being disciplined. In such cases the person needs to be left to their own ways. Paul's advice is that they should be removed from the fellowship of the church. This is sad because the uncorrected attitudes will surely bear their destructive fruit again, and the person in question will be deprived of the blessings of grace that are available to all of God's people.

Fifth, seek and welcome help from trusted friends or counselors who can speak to you and for you. It will be hard to see yourself and events the way others do. You will need help in gaining the perspective of others. It will also be helpful to have another person who can speak for you to those who may find it difficult to hear what you have to say because of their distrust of you.

A final word is in order here. Real change, true repentance, involves the displacing of sinful attitudes and behaviors with godly responses to life. Those who discipline and those who are being disciplined must realize that we change by being filled with the life of Christ not only by being disciplined to empty our lives of the selfish works of the flesh. The goal of the discipline process is to be built up in Christ.

About the Author

James Owen Abrahamson is a ThM graduate of Dallas Theological Seminary and for nearly three decades has been the pastor/teacher of the Chapel Hill Bible Church near the University of North Carolina at Chapel Hill, NC. Though retired from his position at the church, he continues to preach in the Chapel Hill area, write, and teach a regular class at his church.

Jim has served as a church consultant, been a part of the adjunct faculty at UNC's continuing education in religion, and has written and contributed to several books – *Put Your Best Foot Forward* (Abingdon Press, 1994), Quest Study Bible (Zondervan, 1994), *Growing Your Church through Evangelism and Outreach* (Edited by Marshall Shelley, Moorings, 1996), *Lessons in Leadership* (Edited by Randal Roberts, 1999, Kregel), *Peace Seekers* (Light Messages, 2010). He and his wife (Ceecy) have three grown children and four grandchildren.

The passion and theme of Jim's teaching has been "the grace of God" and "the power of Christ's Spirit through the teaching of Scripture" to inspire lives to peace, worship, and service. The theme and content of this book is the heart of much of what he has been saying for three decades of ministry. Jim is committed to a lifestyle of learning, modeling, and teaching to equip believers so they can live authentic Christian lives as ambassadors of God's Kingdom in this world. His website is apttoteach.org. This book is the second of a two part series, which includes a first book *Peace Seekers*.

Subject Index

201

Scripture Index